Vocabulary Drills

EDWARD B. FRY, Ph.D.
Professor Emeritus
Rutgers University

JAMESTOWN PUBLISHERS
Providence, Rhode Island

Vocabulary Drills
Intermediate Level

Catalog No. 770
Copyright © 1986, 1989 by Edward B. Fry

Cover and Text Design by Deborah Hulsey Christie
Cover photograph by Warren Jagger
Illustrations by Richard Bishop

Printed in the United States of America

6 7 8 9 10 HS 96 95 94 93 92

ISBN 0-89061-448-2

CONTENTS

To the Teacher   5

To the Student   9

UNIT 1

1: Meeting Words in Context   14

2: The Roots of Our Language   17

3: Meeting Words in Context   19

4: The Roots of Our Language   22

5: Extending Your Word Power   24

UNIT 2

1: Meeting Words in Context   32

2: The Roots of Our Language   35

3: Meeting Words in Context   37

4: The Roots of Our Language   40

5: Extending Your Word Power   42

UNIT 3

1: Meeting Words in Context   50

2: The Roots of Our Language   53

3: Meeting Words in Context   55

4: The Roots of Our Language   58

5: Extending Your Word Power   60

UNIT 4

1: Meeting Words in Context   68

2: The Roots of Our Language   71

3: Meeting Words in Context   73

4: The Roots of Our Language   76

5: Extending Your Word Power   78

UNIT 5

1: Meeting Words in Context   84

2: The Roots of Our Language   87

3: Meeting Words in Context   89

4: The Roots of Our Language   92

5: Extending Your Word Power   94

UNIT 6

1: Meeting Words in Context   102

2: The Roots of Our Language   105

3: Meeting Words in Context   107

4: The Roots of Our Language   110

5: Extending Your Word Power   112

UNIT 7

1: Meeting Words in Context   120

2: The Roots of Our Language   123

3: Meeting Words in Context   125

4: The Roots of Our Language   128

5: Extending Your Word Power   130

UNIT 8

1: Meeting Words in Context   138

2: The Roots of Our Language   141

3: Meeting Words in Context   143

4: The Roots of Our Language   146

5: Extending Your Word Power   148

UNIT 9

1: Meeting Words in Context   156

2: The Roots of Our Language   159

3: Meeting Words in Context   161

4: The Roots of Our Language   164

5: Extending Your Word Power   166

UNIT 10

1: Meeting Words in Context   174

2: The Roots of Our Language   177

3: Meeting Words in Context   179

4: The Roots of Our Language   182

5: Extending Your Word Power   184

Student Words   191

Answer Key   203

Glossary   223

To the Teacher

Introduction

Is learning vocabulary important? You'd better believe it is! By every measure of common sense, and from research statistics, we know that vocabulary knowledge has a tremendous bearing on reading ability and on most standardized test scores, including those for IQ tests and the SAT.

As long ago as 1916, Lewis Terman, the author of the *Stanford-Binet Tests of Intelligence,* reported a correlation of .91 between the vocabulary section of the test and the total test score. That means that a test-taker's score on the vocabulary section was found to be an accurate predictor of his or her score on the test as a whole. Invariably, those with high vocabulary scores tested high on the entire test. Later studies, done on the *Wechsler Intelligence Scale for Children,* showed correlations that were comparable, though slightly lower. Most major standardized tests—reading achievement tests, college entrance exams (SAT and ACT), graduate school entrance exams (GRE, LSAT, GMAT), and various armed forces selection and placement tests—include a major section on vocabulary.

Vocabulary also plays an extremely important part in reading comprehension. Research by Robert Thorndike has shown that in English-speaking countries such as the United States, England, Scotland and New Zealand there is a correlation of .70 between vocabulary test scores and reading comprehension scores. Vocabulary difficulty is also the most important variable in most of the widely used readability formulas, which are used to calculate the level of difficulty of reading materials.

So, on the basis of solid research results, as well as from a commonsense perspective, it is clear that vocabulary is important. It is a major factor in reading comprehension, and a substantial portion of numerous standardized tests is devoted to the testing of vocabulary knowledge.

Let's spend a minute on the question How large is an average student's vocabulary? This simple question is nearly unanswerable.

First of all, you could ask which vocabulary—reading, writing, listening or speaking. Our *receptive vocabularies,* those that comprise the words we recognize and understand when we hear or read them, tend to be larger than our *expressive vocabularies,* those that comprise the words we use in speaking and writing. The receptive vocabularies of children and young people usually far exceed their expressive vocabularies. In well-educated or well-read adults, the gap is much narrower. This leads us to our first important piece of information related to vocabulary improvement: vocabulary increases through education and through the reading of a wide range of materials.

Let's limit our original big question to How large is a student's *meaning vocabulary?* This encompasses those words whose meanings the student knows, as opposed to *sight vocabulary*— those words that the student recognizes and can pronounce but does not understand.

The results of various research studies vary widely in their estimates of the size of the average student's meaning vocabulary. For example, the lowest estimate for grade seven is 4,600 words, and the high estimate is 51,000. At grade fourteen, which is college sophomore, the range is 7,900 words to 200,000 words. Quite a difference. Part of the discrepancy stems from confusion over what is meant by a "word." Do variant forms constitute different words—are *run, runs* and *running* to be considered different words? Is *ran* different from the other three because its vowel changes? The different decisions that are reached in answer to such questions cause the estimates to differ by several hundred percent. Confusion about how to treat multiple meanings is also a factor that affects estimates. If you understand *run,* as in *Sally can run,* do you automatically understand three other words if you understand the meanings of *run* in the sentences *Sally has a run in her stocking, There is a run on the banks,* and *The fence on the dog run is broken?* The lowest research estimates exclude both variants and multiple meanings, as well as technical and foreign words.

All estimates, however, high or low, reflect constant growth in vocabulary size as students progress through the educational system. As an example, below is some data from the *Basic Word Vocabulary Test* by Harold J. Dupuy, Ph.D.

Grade	Number of Words Known
7	4,600
8	5,300
9	5,900
10	6,400
11	6,700
12	6,900

Note that the table shows greater vocabulary growth in the junior high years than in senior high. This certainly indicates that junior high is a time in which many new words and ideas are being introduced to students, but the apparent difference in growth rate is probably also due to the fact that the test does not reflect the many technical and subject-specific words that senior high school students learn.

An Overview of the Book

The reading selections, lessons and exercises in *Vocabulary Drills* concentrate mainly on two of the best-known and most reliable approaches to vocabulary improvement: the use of context clues and the analysis of the roots of unfamiliar words. Students will learn a fairly large number of words in this book, but, more importantly, they will learn some important skills that will help them to decipher the meanings of new words that they encounter in their own reading.

Context. Sections 1 and 3 of each unit are titled Meeting Words in Context. Each of these sections contains a reading selection that provides the context for five vocabulary words, followed by four exercises. The reading selections have been drawn from sources representing the broad variety of reading materials that students regularly encounter: newspapers, textbooks, general fiction and nonfiction, and reference books. The exercises following the reading selections have two purposes: (1) to develop a student's ability to perceive the meanings of unfamiliar words based on context clues, and (2) to associate the new words encountered in the reading selection with related words and ideas. The latter is accomplished primarily through synonym and antonym exercises and analogies. Such exercises link the new word with words that the student may already know, thereby helping the student retain the word and better understand it.

Student Words. The students are encouraged to find in each reading passage in the Meeting Words in Context sections one or two words that are unfamiliar to them or whose meanings they are uncertain of. They are asked to try to guess from the context of the passage what the words mean, and to write the words and their guess at a definition in a space provided beneath the passage. They are then asked to look up the words in a dictionary and find the correct definitions, and to write the words and definitions in the pages marked Student Words in the back of the book. Through this exercise, the students will be learning to apply to words of their own choosing, some of the skills they are learning in this book.

Roots. Sections 2 and 4 of each unit, which are titled The Roots of Our Language, feature lessons that teach common Greek and Latin roots and some of the English words that contain them. Three exercises related to each lesson drill the roots and the words, and provide students with practice in deciphering unfamiliar words that contain the roots taught in the lesson.

Extension and Review. The fifth and last section of each unit, called Extending Your Word Power, contains five exercises that expand students' understanding of the words that have been taught in the unit. One exercise deals with multiple meanings of selected words, another deals with variant forms of selected words, and a third introduces synonyms for some of the words, and calls for the students to recognize fine distinctions between the synonyms and the vocabulary words. A fourth exercise serves as a review of ten words from the roots lessons, and the fifth and final exercise is a review, usually in game format, that draws on selected vocabulary from both the unit at hand and the previous unit.

Glossary. At the back of the book is a glossary that contains all of the words and roots that are introduced in *Vocabulary Drills*. The definitions given for the words are limited to those meanings that are dealt with in the book. If you would like to expand your students' understanding of any of the words, have them work with a good dictionary and with other word reference books such as a thesaurus and books on usage.

Answer Key. A complete answer key is provided at the back of the book, following the Student Words pages.

How to Use *Vocabulary Drills* in Class

A complete step-by-step guide to the use of *Vocabulary Drills* with your students is contained in the To the Student section, which begins on page 9. You should go through that section with your students, so that they will have a clear understanding of the purpose of the book and of its contents.

Vocabulary Drills has been designed to encourage students to participate completely in the lessons and exercises without fear of making errors. As has been stated previously, the main thrust of the book is on the teaching of skills that will help students learn to build their own vocabularies, and on presenting English as a lively and interesting language, not on the teaching of definitions. Consequently, the book contains no scoring sheets or progress charts. Students should, however, be encouraged to check their answers, to examine their errors and correct them, and to try to figure out why the correct responses are correct. Discussion is also tremendously helpful in learning vocabulary. The more students hear and use new words, the better they will understand the words, learn their fine points of meaning and usage, and remember them. Students should do the exercises on their own, but it

is recommended that, whenever possible, they discuss their responses and correct the exercises as a group. This is especially helpful in the Roots Review exercises in the fifth section of each unit, for those exercises have no specific answers. The students must complete sentences so as to demonstrate their understanding of the meanings of the boldfaced words in the sentence stems. Again, discussion will help the students clarify and refine their understanding of the words.

Vocabulary Extension Activities

This book provides a good starting place for helping your students increase both their receptive and expressive vocabularies. But you can certainly extend the kinds of activities that are presented here, and help your students to increase their vocabularies in many other ways. Following are some suggestions.

(1) *Vocabulary Drills* contains a wide variety of exercise types: multiple-choice, cloze, matching, analogies, substitutions, sentence completion, and a variety of word puzzles and games. You may wish to create similar drills for words of your own choosing. Another effective activity is to challenge your students to create exercise items of their own, using words from their Student Words pages, and to try them out on each other.

(2) Make part of every subject lesson a vocabulary lesson. Whether you are teaching science, grammar or physical education, it is important to teach the specialized vocabulary of the subject. Write any new words on the chalkboard, help students make connections between the new words and subject vocabulary they may already know. Use the new terms in your oral lessons.

(3) Connect new words you teach in as many ways as possible with words and concepts your students are already familiar with. Explore the various meanings of any words that have multiple meanings. Teach any distinctions in meaning,

pronunciation or spelling between homophones and homographs. Generate synonyms and antonyms for the words, if appropriate. Explore the fine distinctions between synonyms, comparing and contrasting them. Present the synonyms in sentences that exhibit their proper use, and encourage your students to generate sentences that use the words appropriately.

(4) Teach your students to categorize new words with other words they know or are learning that deal with the same concept. For example, if you are teaching the word *thyroid,* the students could categorize it with the names of other organs of the body, such as *liver, heart, thymus,* and *kidney.* Have the students label their lists, so the words will be linked in their minds with a concept. Another example: If you are teaching the word COBAL, related words might be FORTRAN, BASIC, and LISP, and the category heading might be Computer Programming Languages.

(5) Teach word continuums related to various concepts with which you are dealing in your subject area. For instance, if you are studying urban communities, and perhaps dealing with the word *metropolis,* you might introduce words related to communities of various sizes and arrange them on the chalkboard in a continuum from smallest community to largest:

hamlet → village → town → city → metropolis → megalopolis

You could then explain the meanings of any words with which the students are unfamiliar, and explore the differences between the various concepts. A metropolis, for instance, is a large city, but it is smaller than a city that is classified as a megalopolis. Also, a megalopolis may encompass several cities, or the highly populated area surrounding an extremely large city. Again, give examples to help your students understand the distinctions between the related concepts.

As a related exercise, you could extend the continuum to a "concept map," drawing lines out from the continuum in a circle and writing words and terms related to the concept. A concept map based on the continuum above, for instance,

might include the terms *county, urban core, transport corridor* and *suburb.*

(6) Explore class/example and coordinate relationships. For example, if you were teaching the word *dictator* and the concept of dictatorship, you could classify a dictator as a ruler, and then bring up other types of rulers. You could then generate a discussion of the various types of rulers, comparing and contrasting them according to their individual properties and characteristics. Interesting class discussions can arise when students are asked to list the ways in which two related concepts are alike and how they are different. Conversely, using *dictator* as a class heading, you could discuss examples of dictators, such as Hitler and Peron, and discuss the similarities and the differences between them.

(7) The most important thing you can do to help your students widen their vocabularies is encourage them to read as much and as widely as possible. Encourage them to explore their interests through reading. Recommend good books and magazine articles to them. Bring in interesting newspaper articles that are relevant to the subjects you are discussing in class, and encourage your students to do the same. Remember that it is almost universally true that good readers have good vocabularies, and that it is difficult to develop a good vocabulary without reading.

Finally, there is one last thing that I would like to stress to you and to your students. Vocabulary development is a lifelong learning necessity. It is very important to success both in school and in life, and it can be a fascinating pursuit as well.

E.F.

I would like to thank the following people for their many valuable contributions to *Vocabulary Drills:*

Dr. Donna Fountoukidis, Montclair State College
Ms. Nancy Schwindinger, Rutgers University
Ms. Katharine M. Archambault
Ms. Lee Teverow

Introduction

Why build your vocabulary?

When you were two or three years old, you knew enough words to express your needs and desires. You could ask for food, say that you wanted to go outside, and insist that you weren't going to eat your peas. By the time you were five or six and began going to school, you knew a lot more words. This was mainly because you'd had many new experiences and learned about new ideas. Every experience and every idea has its own special words attached to it—its own vocabulary. As you began to read, you learned more new ideas through what you read. In that way too, you learned new words and their meanings. Each new subject you have learned in school has introduced you to new words and the ideas attached to them. The result of all this learning is that you have a much larger vocabulary now than you did when you were three. But the process is far from finished.

As you continue in school you will be continuing the process. You will be meeting more and more new ideas and words you can use to talk about those ideas. And the process will continue throughout your life as you read on your own and as you talk with people about their experiences and ideas. We never stop learning. And the more words we know, the more clearly and completely we can express our thoughts and opinions—the more clearly and intelligently we can communicate. So it is important to take every opportunity to build your vocabulary.

The Importance of Reading

The easiest and most natural way to add to your vocabulary is to read as much as you can. Read on a variety of subjects and from many kinds of materials. You will meet many new words that way, and you will become familiar with how the words are used. The more often you meet a word, the better you understand its meaning. The better you understand a word, the more comfortable you will be using it. And the more you use a word, the more likely it is to become a standard part of your working vocabulary. That is how a person's vocabulary grows. If you don't use the new words you learn, you will tend to forget them.

Using Context

The aim of *Vocabulary Drills* is to help you learn how to approach new words and to become more comfortable with the language—free to explore new words and their meanings. In the book you will work with useful vocabulary that is presented in reading selections on many subjects and from many different types of sources. As you read the selections and do the exercises that accompany them, you will be developing your skills in dealing with new words—skills that you can carry over to your own reading. One of the most important skills is learning to use context to get some idea of the meaning of an unfamiliar word. Context is the setting of the word—the ideas in the words and sentences that surround it. A word in a sentence carries an idea that fits in with the whole meaning of the sentence, and of the paragraph in which the sentence is located.

When you are reading on your own and you come across an unfamiliar word, you don't usually want to stop reading to check the word in a dictionary. You should just try to get a fair sense of the word from its context, and keep on reading. You can often come quite close to the meaning of a word by making a guess at it, based on the context. That is a skill you will develop in this book.

Through your work with the exercises, you will also be making the vocabulary words a part of your working vocabulary.

Learning About Roots

Another way by which people build their vocabularies is by learning about the roots of the language—the parts of English words that are based on other, older languages. Many English words are based on word parts borrowed from the ancient Latin and Greek languages. This book contains lessons and exercises that will help you learn the meanings of some Greek and Latin roots and of some words that contain those roots. You can then use your knowledge of roots to help you figure out the meanings of unfamiliar words that you meet in your own reading.

When you have completed this book, you will have learned many new words. More importantly, however, you will have learned how to go on learning new words wherever and whenever you meet them.

How to Use This Book

Vocabulary Drills is divided into ten units. Each unit is divided into five sections. The first and third sections present reading selections followed by exercises related to vocabulary words that are presented in the selections. Sections two and four contain lessons and exercises related to Greek and Latin roots. Section five helps widen your understanding of some of the words you have worked with in the unit, and reviews some of them, as well.

The best way to do the lessons and exercises is to work through them on your own, and then to go over your answers in a group. This gives you the opportunity to use the words aloud and to hear them spoken. Talking about the words and discussing the answers to the exercises will help you better understand the words and how they should be used. Such discussions will help you to become a better speaker and writer.

Now let's examine a unit closely.

Working Through a Unit

Sections 1 and 3: Meeting Words in Context

Reading selections two to three hundred words long begin each of these sections. They contain the vocabulary words you will work with. The selections are taken from many kinds of reading material: newspapers, magazines, general fiction and nonfiction, textbooks and reference materials.

The vocabulary words in each selection appear in boldfaced type. There are five in each passage. As you read a selection, try to figure out the meanings of the boldfaced words from the way they are used. Pay close attention to the ideas contained in the words and sentences that surround each vocabulary word. Try to understand how the vocabulary word fits in with those ideas.

Right below the selection are spaces in which you are to write two words from the passage— *not* the boldfaced words—whose meanings you are not sure of. (Pick two words even if you think you know the meanings of all of them; you may be surprised to learn new things about the words.) Make a guess at the meaning of each word, and write that meaning beside the word. Then compare your definition with the definition given in a dictionary. Be sure to choose the dictionary definition that agrees with the way the word is

used in the reading selection. Check to see how close your definition came to the one given in the dictionary. Finally, enter your two words and their correct definitions on the Student Words pages that begin on page 191.

Four exercises follow each reading selection. Through the exercises you will explore the meanings of the five vocabulary words, *as they are used in the selection.* This is an important point, for, as you know, many words have more than one meaning. In these exercises you will be looking at only the meanings used in the reading selection. There are many different exercise types, including multiple-choice, matching, sentence completion, word substitutions and fill-in-the-blanks. Read the directions for each exercise carefully, to be sure you understand what you are to do.

Each of the exercises deals with the five words from the reading selection. Exercise 1, called Using Context, asks you to try to figure out the meanings of the words from the way they are used in the passage. In Exercises 2, 3 and 4, called Making Connections, you are asked either to match the words with synonyms and antonyms, to match the words with their definitions, to use the words in sentences, or to complete analogies (an analogy is a type of comparison made of word pairs that go together in some way). Work through the exercises on your own. Then, if possible, correct your answers in a group with classmates. Share your answers, talk about the words, and correct any errors you may have made. The Answer Key begins on page 203.

Sections 2 and 4: The Roots of Our Language

A lesson that teaches several Latin and Greek roots and some words that contain those roots begins each of these sections. Following the lesson are three exercises in which you will work with the roots and words that were taught. Exercise 1 is a matching exercise in which you must match five roots and words with their definitions. Exercise 2 is a true-false exercise, containing five statements based on roots and words from the lesson. Exercise 3 may contain questions, fill-in-the-blanks, or a series of multiple-choice questions.

Section 5: Extending Your Word Power

Five exercises make up this section. They build on your understanding of the words you have worked with in the first four parts of the unit. Let's look at each type of exercise.

Multiple Meanings. Many words in the English language have multiple—two or more—meanings. This exercise is based on words from the Meeting Words in Context sections. Each of the words has at least two meanings. You may be asked to find the other meanings of the words in the glossary at the back of the book, or you may be given the other meanings at the beginning of the exercise. In the exercise you will have to choose which of the meanings of the words tell the way the words are used in sentences that are given.

Roots Review. This exercise asks you to complete ten sentences. Each incomplete sentence contains a word you learned about in a Roots Lesson. You must complete the sentence to show that you understand what the word means.

Choosing Just the Right Word. Careful writers and speakers try to choose just the right words to express their ideas. Many words have synonyms—other words that have almost the same meaning. But synonyms rarely mean *exactly* the same thing. Each usually carries its own specific meaning. This exercise has you look closely at words that are very close in meaning but that serve different purposes when it comes to expressing ideas.

Recognizing Other Word Forms. This exercise shows you other forms of some of the words you have studied in the Meeting Words in Context sections of the unit. For instance, if you worked with the word *anticipate* earlier in the unit, this exercise might introduce *anticipation* or *anticipatory*.

Putting Your Vocabulary to Use. This exercise provides a review of some words from the present unit and from the previous unit, as well. This last activity is usually in the form of a game—a word search, a crossword, a bubblegram or the completion of humorous rhyming word pairs.

Checking Your Work

As mentioned earlier, *Vocabulary Drills* contains no grading system or scoring charts. Although you will be adding many new words to your vocabulary as you work in this book, your main goal is *to develop your ability to learn and use words.*

Answer Key. Check your work by using the Answer Key that begins on page 203. Again, we suggest that you go over the exercises in a group. There is, however, no grading involved in *Vocabulary Drills.* The Answer Key is there to allow you to check your answers, not to test you. It takes time to come to a clear understanding of the meaning of a word, so it is expected that you will not always get the right answers to the exercise questions. Just do your best, check your answers, and then go back and try to figure out why the right answer was right. If you are confused by an answer, discuss it with the other members of the group or with your teacher.

Glossary. The Glossary on pages 223–238 contains definitions of all the vocabulary words that have been introduced in the book. Some exercises require the use of the glossary, others suggest that you use it if you cannot recall what a word means. We suggest that you do not use the glossary when you are working on the Using Context exercises in the Meeting Words in Context sections. In those exercises you are being asked to try to figure out the meanings of the words only from the way they are used. Be sure when you consult the glossary that if more than one definition is given for a word you choose the one that gives the meaning you are looking for.

Remember that the more words you know the better you will understand what you read, and the better you will be able to communicate. Good luck!

1: Meeting Words in Context

Reading Selection	Laurel and Hardy: The Early Days
Words Introduced	troupe attain folded seasoned understudy

2: The Roots of Our Language

Roots Introduced	pre- venire con- -dict

3: Meeting Words in Context

Reading Selection	Masters of Comedy
Words Introduced	distinctive graduated decade tribulations cult

4: The Roots of Our Language

Roots Introduced	com- bin- bi- -fort -ple

5: Extending Your Word Power

Multiple Meanings
Roots Review
Using Words Precisely
Recognizing Other Word Forms
Putting Your Vocabulary to Use

1: Meeting Words in Context

Laurel and Hardy: The Early Days

Laurel and Hardy both started out early in show-business, thousands of miles apart. Born in 1890 in England, Laurel, whose real name was Arthur Stanley Jefferson, managed a little theater in his own attic when he was only nine. Oliver Norvell Hardy, born in Georgia in 1892, left home at the age of eight to travel with a **troupe** called Coburn's Minstrels.

By the time they were teenagers, beanpole Stan and butterball Ollie (who already weighed 250 pounds) had discovered that they could make people laugh. Both of them decided to pursue show business careers in earnest. Neither realized that he'd eventually **attain** fame only as part of a team.

Laurel came to the United States as an **understudy** to the great comedian Charlie Chaplin. After their show **folded**, Stan continued in vaudeville, the live variety entertainment of the day, with various partners.

Hardy began his film career in 1913 and Laurel began his in 1917. In those silent-movie days, a producer named Hal Roach was the king of comedy, working with popular comedians of the era. It was he who teamed Laurel and Hardy in 1927. They had already appeared in Hal Roach films together, but not as a team.

Both were **seasoned** performers, but neither was a big star. Laurel was then thirty-seven. Hardy was thirty-five.

Movies were filmed "off the cuff" then—almost made up as shooting went along. Laurel was especially good at inventing slapstick action. It was he who suggested that *The Battle of the Century,* one of Laurel and Hardy's funniest films, feature more pie-throwing than ever. At least 2,000 pies were flung in one long, crazy scene.

Reprinted from *Real World,* with special permission of King Features Syndicate, Inc.

Choose from the story two words that are unfamiliar to you or whose meanings you are not completely sure of. (Do not choose words that appear in boldfaced type.) Write the words on the lines provided below. Then, beside each word, write what you think it means, based on how it was used in the story.

1. _____ : _____

   _____

2. _____ : _____

   _____

When you have finished the exercises in this lesson, go to your dictionary and find the definitions for the words you entered above. If a word has more than one meaning, look for the one that defines the word as it is used in the story. Then write the words and their dictionary definitions in the Student Words pages at the back of the book. How close did you come to figuring out their meanings for yourself?

Put an *x* in the box beside each correct answer. For clues to the meanings of the words, reread the parts of the passage in which the words appear.

1. From the name of the troupe Hardy traveled with as a child, you can tell that **troupe** means
   □ a. a motorcycle gang.
   □ b. boy scouts.
   □ c. a group of performers.
   □ d. a big, fancy car.

2. To **attain** fame means to
   □ a. wish to be famous.
   □ b. try to become famous without success.
   □ c. think little of fame.
   □ d. succeed in becoming famous.

3. The sentence in which **folded** appears might have been written: Stan continued in vaudeville after Chaplin's show
   □ a. closed.   □ c. went overseas.
   □ b. returned.   □ d. got better.

4. From what is told of the careers of Laurel and Hardy before the word *seasoned* appears, you can guess that a **seasoned** performer is one who
   □ a. performs only during a certain season.
   □ b. takes only certain kinds of roles.
   □ c. has become a big star.
   □ d. has gained experience over time.

5. As **understudy** to Charlie Chaplin, Laurel
   □ a. filled in for Chaplin if he couldn't perform.
   □ b. carried Chaplin's makeup and costumes.
   □ c. studied with Chaplin.
   □ d. had the dressing room directly under Chaplin's.

1:2 Making Connections

For each boldfaced vocabulary word in the sentences below, choose a synonym or an antonym from the list that follows. Write the synonyms and antonyms in the blanks.

experienced   substitute   gain   group   closed

lose   individual   untried   opened   competitor

1. Hardy left home at the age of eight to travel with a **troupe** called Coburn's Minstrels.

   synonym: _____   **antonym:** _____

2. Neither realized that he'd eventually **attain** fame only as part of a team.

   synonym: _____   **antonym:** _____

3. Laurel came to the United States as **understudy** to the great comedian Charlie Chaplin.

   synonym: _____   **antonym:** _____

4. After their show **folded**, Stan continued in vaudeville with various partners.

   synonym: _____   **antonym:** _____

5. Both were **seasoned** performers, but neither was a big star.

   synonym: _____   **antonym:** _____

1:3 Making Connections

Complete the following analogies by inserting one of the five vocabulary words in the blank at the end of each one. Remember that in an analogy the last two words or phrases must be related to each other in the same way that the first two are related. The colon in an analogy is read "is to," and the symbol : : is read "as." So "high: low: : wide: narrow" would be read "high is to low as wide is to narrow."

troupe   attain   understudy   folded   seasoned

1. teacher: substitute: : actor: _____

2. retreated: advanced: : opened: _____

3. embrace: hold: : reach: _____

4. beginner: inexperienced: : veteran: _____

5. athlete: team: : performer: _____

1:4 Making Connections

Complete each sentence with the correct vocabulary word.

troupe   attain   understudy   folded   seasoned

1. Greta hoped to _____ the next level of expertise in karate by the end of the year.

2. A _____ chef can easily whip up a complicated sauce that a beginner would find difficult to make.

3. Ricardo was extremely nervous during his audition for a spot in his favorite dance _____ .

4. Many neighborhood shoppers were saddened when the corner grocery store _____ after twenty-three years in business.

5. Although Esther had never played Juliet on stage, she knew the lines because she had been an _____ to the actress who played the role on Broadway.

2: The Roots of Our Language

pre-

Since we are studying prefixes, let's look at the word *prefix,* which means, literally, the part of the word that is fixed before the root. *Pre-* means before. It forms the beginning of many common English words. For instance, as you probably know, *prehistoric* means before the time when people started writing about the events of their times—before written history. *Preatomic* refers to the time before the use of atomic energy and the atom bomb. *Precook* means to cook part way before finally cooking, or before reheating.

A word that appears often in the news and in history books is *prejudice.* It means to form an opinion without taking the time and care to judge fairly— to judge before knowing all the facts. *From stories he heard about crooked lawyers, Nathan formed a prejudice against all lawyers.*

To preclude (pree-KLUDE) means to shut out or rule out in advance—to prevent or make impossible: *The fact that Harry plays football on weekday afternoons precludes his taking piano lessons after school.* The *clude* comes from a Latin word meaning to close or to shut out.

venire

con-

A word that is close to *preclude* in meaning is *prevent,* which means to keep from happening, or to hold or keep back. The *vent* part of the word comes from the root *venire,* which means to come. With the *pre-* prefix on that root, we get "to come before." The root *venire* also forms the basis for the word *convention.* Since the prefix *con-* means together, combining it with the root gives us the meaning to come together. And that is just what a convention is—a gathering of people for a particular purpose. Large organizations often have annual conventions at which they share ideas and news about the business or interests they share. *Convention* also is a synonym for *custom,* which is the generally agreed upon behavior of a group of people. Men, for instance, observe convention by not wearing hats in restaurants.

-dict

To get back to *pre-,* let's look at the word *predict.* To predict something is to tell in advance that it is going to happen: *Some people claim that they can predict the future.* The root *-dict* means say. It is also the root of the word *diction,* which refers to a person's manner of expressing ideas in words—a style of speaking or writing. Good diction is the ability to choose words carefully and to express ideas clearly.

If you stand ahead of other people in a line, you precede them. Also, youth precedes old age. *Precede* means to go before in time or order. Don't confuse *precede* with *proceed,* which means to move forward or to carry on with an activity. When you are driving a car and you come to a stop sign, you must stop before you proceed across the intersection. *Don't let me interrupt you; proceed with what you were doing.*

To wrap up, let's look at the word *precognition. Precognition* means knowing about something before it happens. *Cognition* means knowing. If you have cognition about something, you know about it. And if you don't want to be recognized, you might want to travel incognito, or in disguise. *In* and *cognito* together mean unknown. *Incognito* means with one's identity hidden.

2:1 Write each word or root listed on the left beside its meaning on the right.

pre-

prejudice

con-

diction

precede

1. _____ to judge before knowing the facts

2. _____ before

3. _____ to go before

4. _____ together

5. _____ manner of expressing ideas in words

2:2 Mark each statement as either true or false.

_____ 1. To precede someone is to go after him.

_____ 2. Since *con-* means together and *vent* comes from a root that means to come, a convention is a coming together of a group of people.

_____ 3. If you have good diction, you express ideas well in words.

_____ 4. If you have formed a prejudice against someone, you have done so only after examining all the facts.

_____ 5. To precook food is to cook it again after it has been cooked once.

2:3 Answer the following questions.

1. If you prepay for a mail-order purchase, do you pay when you send in the order, or when the purchased item arrives? _____

_____

2. If you form an opinion by prejudging, you are likely to develop a _____ .

3. Considering the fact that the root *dict-* means to say, what do you think happens when a person dictates a letter into a tape recorder? _____

_____

4. If you know that *con-* means together and *greg* means a crowd of people, what do you think *congregate* means? _____

_____

5. A person who foretells the future, or says what is going to happen, does what? _____

_____

3:Meeting Words in Context

Masters of Comedy

With their **distinctive** voices, Laurel and Hardy moved easily from silent movies into the "talkies." They remained popular through the Great Depression, which started in 1929 and lasted for about ten years. Americans may have been down-and-out, but they still needed entertainment.

The team **graduated** from two-reel films to full-length features. In all, they appeared together in seventy-seven shorts and twenty-eight feature films. Students of film say their best work was done in the 1920s and 1930s.

For **decades** more, the public enjoyed the derby-hatted duo, who faced more **tribulations** in two reels than most of us face in a year.

Surprisingly, the critics of their day didn't regard Stan and Ollie as great artists. Today, however, the tearful Laurel and the tie-twirling Hardy are considered important contributors to film comedy.

"Well, here's another fine mess you've gotten me into, Stanley," Ollie would whine. You could analyze their art for hours, and many scholars have. But the main thing is to just sit back and enjoy them.

Offscreen, Laurel and Hardy had separate interests and separate lives. But each admired the comedic artistry of the other.

After their retirement from films, the two toured abroad. Europeans loved them. In the United States today, a Laurel and Hardy **cult** still carries the torch of admiration for the two master zanies.

Oliver Hardy died in 1957, and Stan Laurel in 1965.

Reprinted from *Real World*, with special permission of King Features Syndicate, Inc.

Choose from the story two words that are unfamiliar to you or whose meanings you are not completely sure of. (Do not choose words that appear in boldfaced type.) Write the words on the lines provided below. Then, beside each word, write what you think it means, based on how it was used in the story.

1. _____ : _____

_____

2. _____ : _____

_____

When you have finished the exercises in this lesson, go to your dictionary and find the definitions for the words you entered above. If a word has more than one meaning, look for the one that defines the word as it is used in the story. Then write the words and their dictionary definitions in the Student Words pages at the back of the book. How close did you come to figuring out their meanings for yourself?

3:1 Using Context

Below are five sentence from the reading passage. From the four answer choices that follow each sentence, choose the one that gives the best definition of the boldfaced word in the sentence. Put an *x* in the box beside it. Use the context, or setting, provided by the sentence to help you discover the meaning of the word. If the sentence itself does not provide enough clues to the word, go back to the passage and read the paragraph in which the sentence appears.

1. With their **distinctive** voices, Laurel and Hardy moved easily from silent movies into the "talkies."
   - ☐ a. loud
   - ☐ b. unpleasant
   - ☐ c. ordinary
   - ☐ d. unusual

2. The team **graduated** from two-reel films to full-length features.
   - ☐ a. got diplomas
   - ☐ b. moved to a higher level
   - ☐ c. alternated between
   - ☐ d. slowly got used to

3. For **decades** more, the public enjoyed the derby-hatted duo, who faced more tribulations in two reels than most of us face in a year.
   - ☐ a. periods of ten years
   - ☐ b. hundreds of days
   - ☐ c. periods of twenty years
   - ☐ d. an unknown period of time

4. For decades more, the public enjoyed the derby-hatted duo, who faced more **tribulations** in two reels than most of us face in a year.
   - ☐ a. movie directors
   - ☐ b. voice teachers
   - ☐ c. difficulties
   - ☐ d. good times or fun

5. In the United States today, a Laurel and Hardy **cult** still carries the torch of admiration for the two master zanies.
   - ☐ a. fan
   - ☐ b. group of admirers
   - ☐ c. actors magazine
   - ☐ d. memorial statue

3:2 Making Connections

In this exercise, the list of vocabulary words is followed by definitions of the words as they are used in the reading passage. Write each word in front of its definition.

distinctive   graduated   decade   tribulations   cult

1. _____ : great troubles or distress

2. _____ : passed from one level to a higher one

3. _____ : group showing great admiration

4. _____ : period of ten years

5. _____ : special; recognizably different

3:3 Making Connections

Listed below are five vocabulary words from the reading passage, followed by ten words and phrases that are related to them in some way. They may be synonyms, antonyms or definitions. On the line next to each word or phrase, write the vocabulary word that is related to it.

distinctive   graduated   decade   tribulations   cult

1. progressed _____

2. difficulties _____

3. ordinary _____

4. woes _____

5. opponents _____

6. ten years _____

7. happy events _____

8. went backwards _____

9. group of followers _____

10. special _____

3:4 Making Connections

Complete each sentence with the correct vocabulary word.

distinctive   graduated   decade   tribulations   cult

1. Greg could still remember the day he _____ from his tricycle to a twenty-inch bicycle with training wheels.

2. The girls talked for hours about the _____ of their favorite soap-opera characters.

3. The candy store had a _____ aroma of chocolate, licorice and newsprint, all mixed together.

4. Years after his death, there is still a large _____ interested in the music and style of Elvis Presley.

5. Nora spent a lot of time daydreaming about exciting events she hoped would take place in her life over the next _____ .

4: The Roots of Our Language

com- The prefix *com-* can mean together, with or thoroughly. The word *combine,* for instance, means to bring two or more things together to form a new thing. To make cookies, a baker combines all the necessary ingredients. The two chemical elements oxygen and hydrogen are combined in water. The *bine* part of *combine* comes from the Latin word *bini,* meaning "two by two."

bin-
bi- *Bini-* is often seen in English words as the prefixes *bin-* and *bi-,* both meaning two. A bicycle, for instance, is a two-wheeled vehicle, a two-hundredth anniversary is a bicentennial, and something that is binary is made up of two parts. The binary number system is based on only two numbers, 0 and 1. That number system forms the basis for computers.

-fort In the word *comfort* we meet the root *-fort,* which, as you might expect, means strong. A fort is a strong, or fortified, place. To offer comfort is to bring someone strength and hope—to offer cheer. Something that is comfortable gives physical comfort—ease, contentment, security. In music we meet the word *forte,* which means in a loud or forceful manner. Such a notation on a piece of sheet music indicates that the performer is to play that passage loudly.

Are you sometimes asked to write a composition? *Composition,* as you might imagine, comes from *compose,* which means to put together. A story is composed by combining ideas, works of art are composed by combining elements of design, music is composed by combining notes. A person who composes music is called a composer. The result of composing is a composition.

Something that is made of separate parts is called a composite (cum-PAHZ-ut). When a victim describes a criminal to the police, a police artist sometimes draws a composite picture of the criminal, based on the description of individual characteristics—type of nose, hair style, shape of eyes, and so on.

In the field of electronics and engineering, we talk about components. They are the individual parts that go into a product. A keyboard, for instance, is one component of a computer terminal. A component stereo system is built by combining individual parts, such as speakers, a turntable and a tuner, often of different makes. In chemistry or pharmacy, the products that are made by combining individual elements are called compounds.

-ple Finally, let us complete this discussion of *com-*. *Complete* means finished, whole or full. The *-ple* root means fill, so *complete* literally means with fullness. This might help you to remember the difference between two words that people often confuse: *complement* and *compliment*. Notice that *complement* has the root *-ple*. A complement is the amount needed to fill or complete something: *A blue scarf would be the perfect complement to that outfit. Compliment* sounds the same but has a different meaning. To compliment a person is to give praise.

4:1 Write each word or root listed on the left beside its meaning on the right.

bi- 1. _____ two

bicentennial 2. _____ in a loud or forceful manner

forte 3. _____ two-hundredth anniversary

compose 4. _____ finished, whole or full

complete 5. _____ to put together

4:2 Mark each statement as either true or false.

_____ 1. The United States celebrated its bicentennial in 1976, two hundred years after the country declared its independence from England.

_____ 2. To give someone a complement is to tell him something nice about himself.

_____ 3. When you compose your written assignments, you put together your ideas, then write them down.

_____ 4. Since *lateral* refers to side, if two nations sign a peace treaty that they both will honor, they are signing a bilateral agreement.

_____ 5. The notation *forte* on a piece of sheet music tells the pianist to play fast.

4:3 Answer the following questions.

1. If you know that a manual task is one that must be done by hand, what do you think a bimanual task is? _____

_____

2. When you are upset and someone tells you to "pull yourself together," or to "get yourself together," they are telling you to _____ yourself.

3. If you know that *ped* means foot, what is an animal that is a biped? _____

_____

4. In order for this sentence to be finished, you have to _____ it by filling in the blank.

5. What number system forms the basis for computers? _____

5:Extending Your Word Power

5:1 Multiple Meanings

Some of the vocabulary words you met in this unit have more than one meaning. Those words and their definitions are listed below. Begin by reading the definitions for each word.

Next to each sentence that follows, write the letter of the definition that gives the meaning of the vocabulary word as it is used in the sentence.

graduate

a. (v.) finish a course of study at a school

b. (v.) pass from one stage or level to a higher one

c. (v.) mark out in equal spaces for measuring

seasoned

a. (v.) improved the flavor of

b. (adj.) grown experienced over a period of time

c. (v.) made fit or became fit by treatment or aging

fold

a. (v.) bend or double over on itself

b. (v.) bring to an end; go out of business

_____ 1. The soup was delicious, **seasoned** with just the right combination of fresh herbs from the garden.

_____ 2. The track is **graduated** in ten-yard sections, so runners can easily calculate their speed and distance.

_____ 3. After three summers as a stock boy at the supermarket, Lloyd finally **graduated** to the position of clerk.

_____ 4. The roller-skating rink **folded** without warning; one day it was filled with skaters, and the next a For Sale sign was posted on it.

_____ 5. A cast-iron skillet should be **seasoned** with oil every few months to ensure a smooth, slippery surface for cooking.

_____ 6. Before he raced off to soccer practice, William **folded** his shirts and put them into the drawer.

_____ 7. Irene was genuinely surprised to find out that she would **graduate** from college with the highest honors.

5:2 Roots Review

The incomplete sentences below contain words that you learned in the two roots lessons in this unit. Complete each sentence so that it makes sense and shows the meaning of the boldfaced vocabulary word.

1. The blue paint was **combined** _____ _____ .

2. In an attempt to offer **comfort**, Frank _____ _____ .

3. Joan studied the **binary** number system so that she _____ _____ .

4. The imaginary animal that Zac created in art class was a **composite** of _____ _____ .

5. Professor Upunhyer explained that in **preatomic** times _____ _____ .

6. In preparing for the **convention**, the hotel management _____ _____ .

7. "If this meat has been **precooked**," Elmer began, "then _____ _____ ."

8. The actor tried to make the trip **incognito**, but _____ _____ .

9. The bad weather **prevented** Ron _____ _____ .

10. From the way he spoke, it was clear that John was **prejudiced** _____ _____ .

5:3 Choosing Just the Right Word

Many of the words in this unit have a number of synonyms. In some cases the synonyms are slightly different in meaning. In this exercise, synonym studies are provided for two of the vocabulary words. Use either the vocabulary words or their synonyms to complete the sentences in the exercise. Refer to the synonym studies as you decide which choice carries the best meaning for the specific context of each sentence. The word in the sentence may appear in a different tense than it does in the study.

attain   acquire

The words *attain* and *acquire* both mean to gain or reach. *Attain* is used when speaking of accomplishment or of reaching a particular state of being. *She attained her goal. The man had attained the ripe old age of ninety. Acquire* means to come into possession of a material object or a personality trait or characteristic by any number of different means. *Morgan acquired a limp in his youth. Upon the death of her grandfather, Kate acquired his estate.*

1. Penelope could not remember how she had _____ the antique oriental vase on the table in her parlor.

2. Maureen worked hard to _____ the balance she wanted between her social life and her studies.

3. Over the years, Hernandez _____ an annoying habit of clicking his teeth after every few words of conversation.

4. The leaders of the two nations were responsible to their people for finding a way to _____ peace.

distinctive   peculiar

Distinctive and *peculiar* both indicate a special quality. A distinctive quality is one that is noticeably different and uncommon. It is also often special in the sense of being superior or worthy of notice. *Her paintings had a distinctive brightness. Peculiar* applies to qualities belonging only to an individual, a group or a certain kind of thing. It stresses the unusualness of the quality and sometimes implies strangeness or oddness as well. *He spoke in an accent peculiar to the eastern hills of Tennessee.*

5. The house was painted a _____ shade of blue, which gave it a stately, handsome look.

6. Roy's dog had a _____ odor that made him unpopular among the neighborhood's pets.

7. In Tibet, archaeologists found remnants of cave paintings _____ to an ancient tribe of nomads.

8. The actor was known for his romantic good looks and _____ walk.

5:4 Recognizing Other Word Forms
The words listed below are other forms of the vocabulary words you have worked with in this unit. Fill in the blank in each sentence with the appropriate word. Use what you learned about the vocabulary in the unit to help you figure out what these words mean. If you need more help, refer to the glossary.

attainment   graduation   folding   distinction   attainable

1. The naked eye is not capable of seeing the _____ between minute differences in size.

2. Paul's main goal was the _____ of a degree in architecture.

3. For the first time in her ten long years of training, Michelle believed that her dream of becoming a distinguished opera singer was _____.

4. The discouraged partners racked their brains trying to think of something that might keep their catering business from _____.

5. Greg intended to take a vacation after _____, before starting his search for a job.

5:5 Putting Your Vocabulary to Use

Each word scramble below is followed by a definition or synonym of the scrambled word. Use the definition or synonym as a clue to help you unscramble the word. Write the word in the space provided. The circled letters will combine to form a phrase related to Laurel and Hardy's comic style. Write the phrase on the line provided at the bottom.

1. OMEPSCO   formulate   _ _ _ _ _ ◯ _

2. NIBORUTILAT   distress   _ _ _ _ _ ◯ _ _ _ _

3. CADEED   ten years   _ _ _ ◯ _ _

4. CREPDEE   go ahead of   ◯ _ _ _ _ _ _

5. DTUENDRYSU   substitute   _ _ _ _ _ ◯ _ _ _

6. TODIICN   pronunciation   _ _ _ ◯ _ _ _

7. BNOCMEI   blend   _ _ _ _ ◯ _ _

8. RAQECUI   get   _ ◯ _ _ _ _ _

9. OPERKCO   cook ahead   _ _ _ _ _ _ ◯

10. RTPIHEOSRCI   before written history   _ _ _ ◯ _ _ _ _ _ _ _

11. POTERU   acting company   _ _ _ ◯ _ _

12. OLTECMPE   finish   _ _ ◯ _ _ _ _ _

13. NEDSSAOE   experienced   _ _ _ _ ◯ _ _ _

14. ERALIPUC   odd   _ _ _ _ _ _ _ ◯

Phrase: _____

 *alindromes*

Backward and forward they read the same. They get their name from the Greek word *palindromos,* meaning "running back again." A palindrome may consist of a single word, such as *madam,* or of a phrase or sentence—Madam, I'm Adam.

People who enjoy playing with words have been making up palindromes for thousands of years. A famous Greek palindrome that appears around many water fountains reads

NIΨONANOMHMATAMHMONANOΨIN

meaning "Wash my transgressions, not only my face."

Below are a few well-known palindromes. In the last one, each word is a palindrome, as well. Can you compose a palindrome of your own?

Step on no pets.

A man, a plan, a canal—Panama.

Never odd or even.

Anna: "Did Otto peep?" Otto: "Did Anna?"

1: Meeting Words in Context

Reading Selection   Cat Communication

Words Introduced   originate   direct   indicate   posture submissive

2: The Roots of Our Language

Roots Introduced   ad-   -here   minister   -jac   -jec   apt   opt

3: Meeting Words in Context

Reading Selection   Caring for a Cat

Words Introduced   remedy   eliminate   confine   discipline reduce

4: The Roots of Our Language

Roots Introduced   dis-   aster   -logy   orient   lodge

5: Extending Your Word Power

Multiple Meanings
Roots Review
Using Words Precisely
Recognizing Other Word Forms
Putting Your Vocabulary to Use

1: Meeting Words in Context

Cat Communication

Cats communicate with one another, with other animals, and with human beings in a variety of ways. Cats use sounds, body signals, and scents as means of communication.

Some experts estimate that a cat can make more than 60 different sounds, ranging from a soft purr to a loud wail, or *caterwaul*. Most of these sounds **originate** in the *larynx* (voice box) in the throat. But some scientists believe purring arises from vibrations in the wall of a blood vessel in the chest. The vibrations result when the speed of the blood flow increases.

The sounds a cat makes may have various meanings. For example, depending on the situation, a meow can be a friendly greeting, or it may express curiosity, hunger, or loneliness. Purring usually means contentment, but some cats also purr when they are sick. Hisses, growls, and screams **indicate** anger and fear.

Cats also communicate through various body and tail positions and facial expressions. A contented cat often lies on its chest with its eyes half closed. To invite play or petting, some cats roll over on one side and wave a paw in the air. However, a similar **posture** accompanied by extended claws, a **direct** stare, and ears folded back indicates a fearful cat ready to defend itself. A friendly cat may greet someone with its tail raised vertically. It may also bump its head against the person and lick an extended hand. An angry or frightened cat flicks its tail from side to side, arches its back, and puffs up its fur. A **submissive** cat crouches down, flattens its ears, and avoids direct eye contact.

Excerpted from *The World Book Encyclopedia.* © 1985 World Book, Inc.

Choose from the story two words that are unfamiliar to you or whose meanings you are not completely sure of. (Do not choose words that appear in boldfaced type.) Write the words on the lines provided below. Then, beside each word, write what you think it means, based on how it was used in the story.

1. _____ : _____

   _____

2. _____ : _____

   _____

When you have finished the exercises in this lesson, go to your dictionary and find the definitions for the words you entered above. If a word has more than one meaning, look for the one that defines the word as it is used in the story. Then write the words and their dictionary definitions in the Student Words pages at the back of the book. How close did you come to figuring out their meanings for yourself?

1:1 Using Context

Below are five sentences from the reading passage. From the four answer choices that follow each sentence, choose the one that gives the best definition of the boldfaced word. Put an x in the box beside it. Use the context, or setting, provided by the sentence to help you discover the meaning of the word. If the sentence itself does not provide enough clues, go back to the passage and read the paragraph in which the sentence appears.

1. Most of these sounds **originate** in the larynx (voice box) in the throat.
   - ☐ a. grow
   - ☐ b. begin
   - ☐ c. continue
   - ☐ d. stay

2. However, a similar posture accompanied by extended claws, a **direct** stare, and ears folded back indicates a fearful cat ready to defend itself.
   - ☐ a. straightforward
   - ☐ b. timid
   - ☐ c. brief
   - ☐ d. unsteady

3. Hisses, growls, and screams **indicate** anger and fear.
   - ☐ a. eliminate
   - ☐ b. take the place of
   - ☐ c. cause
   - ☐ d. are a sign of

4. However, a similar **posture** accompanied by extended claws, a direct stare, and ears folded back indicates a fearful cat ready to defend itself.
   - ☐ a. game
   - ☐ b. greeting
   - ☐ c. body position
   - ☐ d. walk

5. A **submissive** cat crouches down, flattens its ears, and avoids direct eye contact.
   - ☐ a. yielding to authority
   - ☐ b. poorly trained
   - ☐ c. excited and playful
   - ☐ d. sick

1:2 Making Connections

Listed below are the five vocabulary words from the reading passage, followed by fourteen words and phrases that are related to them in some way. They may be synonyms, antonyms or definitions. On the line next to each word or phrase, write the vocabulary word that is related to it.

originate   direct   indicate   posture   submissive

1. signify _____

2. rebellious _____

3. bold _____

4. stance _____

5. gives in easily _____

6. start out _____

7. steady _____

8. sidelong _____

9. point out _____

10. end up _____

11. obedient _____

12. position _____

13. show _____

14. aggressive _____

1:3 Making Connections

Complete the following analogies by inserting one of the five vocabulary words in the blank at the end of each one. In an analogy, the last two words or phrases must be related to each other in the same way that the first two are related. The colon in an analogy is read "is to," and the symbol : : is read "as." So "high : low : : wide : narrow" would be read "high is to low as wide is to narrow."

originate   direct   indicate   posture   submissive

1. wave : greet : : point : _____

2. happy : gleeful : : humble : _____

3. curved : straight : : roundabout : _____

4. accept : reject : : end : _____

5. face : expression : : body : _____

1:4 Making Connections

Complete each sentence with the correct vocabulary word.

originated   direct   indicate   posture   submissive

1. Gloria's erect _____ makes her appear taller than she actually is.

2. Manny asked a _____ question and was rewarded with an equally straightforward answer.

3. Randy, a _____ child, climbed the fence when his brother told him to, even though he was scared.

4. The signal beside the tracks turned yellow to _____ that a train was approaching.

5. The cacao tree, from whose seeds chocolate and cocoa are made, _____ in the West Indies.

2: The Roots of Our Language

ad-

The prefix *ad-* means toward or to. We see this common prefix in *adhere* (ad-HERE), which means to stick fast or to cling. Darts with suction cups adhere to the dart board. You use glue to adhere things that you want to stay together. *Adhere* also means to support a person or an idea—to be loyal. For example, someone who adheres to certain beliefs and principles sticks by them: *In England the Puritans adhered to their religious beliefs in spite of*

-here

persecution. The root *-here* comes from a Latin word meaning to stick. *Adhesive* comes from the same root. You have certainly used adhesive tape, which is tape that sticks to almost anything. Tape that has good adhesion sticks well, or firmly. Tape with poor adhesion, such as masking tape, does not stick well. A related word, which applies to people who exhibit stick-to-itiveness, is *adherent* (ad-HERE-unt). An adherent is a person who adheres, or believes strongly in and sticks by a particular leader, cause or idea. Political and religious leaders often have adherents—followers who strongly support them.

minister

An administrator is someone who manages or directs an organization. In schools, the principal and vice principal are administrators. The root *minister* comes from the Latin word for servant. Today a minister is a member of the clergy (those ordained for religious work) and is sometimes referred to as a "servant of God." A minister may also be a person who is given charge of a department of the government. The Minister of Transportation, for instance, is in charge of the Department of Transportation. A foreign minister is a person who is sent to a foreign country to represent his or her own government. Your school administrators are servants of the school board, and in their professional positions they also serve the teachers and students so that the education program can be successful.

-jac
-jec

The word *adjacent* (uh-JASE-unt) means to lie next to or close by. You live adjacent to your next-door neighbor. The root *-jac* or *-jec* means lie, so buildings that are adjacent are, literally, lying next to each other. If the drug store is adjacent to the laundromat, the two businesses are side by side.

apt

It is fitting that we now consider the word *adapt*. The root *apt* means to fit. To adapt something is to make it fit, often by modifying it to some extent: *The boys adapted the wheels from an old tricycle to fit the go-cart they were making.* The change that is made to make a thing fit a new purpose or space is called an adaptation. *Adaptation* is also used to refer to the ways in which animals develop to suit their specific environments. Web feet, for example, is an adaptation of waterfowl that makes them fit to swim as well as to walk. *Apt* is also a word in itself. It means fitting or appropriate: *Mary's apt reply showed that she had truly understood the question. Apt* also means likely: *If you do not measure carefully, you are apt to make a mistake.*

opt

In the word *adopt,* the root *opt* means to choose. You have probably usually heard this word in the context of adopting a child. People who adopt a child choose to raise as their own a child who was born to other people. But *adopt* has a broader meaning than that. It may mean to take on. A person may, for instance, adopt an attitude: *Fred didn't want to show that he was scared, so he adopted an attitude of confidence. Adopt* may also mean to formally accept or approve. When the U.S. Congress approves a bill, we say that they have adopted it.

2:1 Write each word or root listed on the left beside its meaning on the right.

adhere   1. _____ to take on

minister   2. _____ to stick fast or to cling

adjacent   3. _____ fitting or appropriate

apt   4. _____ next to or close by

adopt   5. _____ servant

2:2 Mark each statement as either true or false.

_____ 1. If your house and your best friend's house are adjacent, you are next-door neighbors.

_____ 2. To adopt something is to make it fit.

_____ 3. If you make a fool of yourself with a statement that was not well thought out, the statement was probably apt.

_____ 4. Ministers work only for religious institutions.

_____ 5. Adherents of an idea are those people who oppose the idea.

2:3 Put an *x* in front of the answer choice you think is correct.

1. If someone who was shy and quiet suddenly becomes outgoing, it could be said that she has

☐ a. adopted a new   ☐ b. adhered to   ☐ c. adapted to a
    lifestyle.   her ways.   quiet life.

2. A servant of the church would be called a

☐ a. principal.   ☐ b. president.   ☐ c. minister.

3. A remark that is just right in a particular social situation could be said to be

☐ a. apt.   ☐ b. opt.   ☐ c. adapted.

4. Flies stick to flypaper because the paper is coated with a substance that makes them

☐ a. sick.   ☐ b. fit.   ☐ c. adhere.

5. Two countries located on either side of the same border are

☐ a. adherents.   ☐ b. adjacent.   ☐ c. parallel.

3: Meeting Words in Context

Caring for a Cat

Cats are clean animals and easy to housebreak. To train a cat to use a litter box, one must watch the animal carefully. When it begins to wander searchingly from one place to another, it must be put into the litter box. The litter must be changed often, and the pan should be washed with soap and water every few days.

A cat likes to exercise its claws by digging them into or scratching furniture. A scratching post helps to **reduce** damage to furniture. A piece of wood covered with carpeting makes a good scratching post. Every time the cat claws at the furniture, it should be taken to the post, until it learns to use it on its own.

Most cats refuse to be **disciplined**, although they may understand "no." They learn their names quickly, however, and many will come when called. If a cat is shown a trick that it likes, it will learn to do it.

Cats should be **confined** to the house, especially at night. Cats that are allowed to roam disturb the neighbors with their crying and fighting. A female cat should never be allowed to roam during her mating season.

Proper care usually will **eliminate** the threat of disease. Unusual symptoms or behavior should be watched for, and the animal should be taken to the veterinarian on a regular basis. A cat should be vaccinated early against rabies and other serious diseases.

A cat will clean itself by licking its fur. As it licks itself, it will swallow hairs that eventually form feltlike balls in its stomach and intestines. Although daily brushing cuts down on hair balls, some will form anyway. A veterinarian can prescribe a **remedy** to help a cat eliminate the hair.

Lastly, a cat should never be dropped or thrown, as it can be seriously injured. Contrary to popular belief, cats do not always land on their feet.

Choose from the story two words that are unfamiliar to you or whose meanings you are not completely sure of. (Do not choose words that appear in boldfaced type.) Write the words on the lines provided below. Then, beside each word, write what you think it means, based on how it was used in the story.

1. _____ : _____

   _____

2. _____ : _____

   _____

When you have finished the exercises in this lesson, go to your dictionary and find the definitions for the words you entered above. If a word has more than one meaning, look for the one that defines the word as it is used in the story. Then write the words and their dictionary definitions in the Student Words pages at the back of the book. How close did you come to figuring out their meanings for yourself?

3:1 Using Context

Put an *x* in the box beside each correct answer. For clues to the meanings of the words, reread the parts of the passage in which the words appear.

1. From the sentence in which *remedy* appears in the story, you can tell that a **remedy** prescribed by a veterinarian is a
   ☐ a. friend. ☐ c. hairbrush.
   ☐ b. medication. ☐ d. special exercise.

2. To "**eliminate** the threat" of disease or injury means to
   ☐ a. get rid of the possibility.
   ☐ b. lessen the seriousness.
   ☐ c. change the course.
   ☐ d. increase the chances.

3. A cat who is "**confined** to the house" is one that
   ☐ a. doesn't have a home.
   ☐ b. doesn't like to go outside.
   ☐ c. is sick.
   ☐ d. is not allowed to go outside.

4. The second part of the sentence in which **disciplined** appears helps you to understand that in this context the word means
   ☐ a. trained to obey.
   ☐ b. put out of the house.
   ☐ c. punished.
   ☐ d. yelled at.

5. The sentence in which the word **reduce** appears tells you that if you provide a scratching post for your cat, damage to your furniture will be
   ☐ a. repaired.
   ☐ b. lessened.
   ☐ c. increased.
   ☐ d. delayed.

3:2 Making Connections

Complete the following analogies by inserting one of the five vocabulary words in the blank at the end of each one. Remember that in an analogy, the last two words or phrases must be related in the same way that the first two are related.

remedy   eliminate   confine   discipline   reduce

1. make worse : improve : : create : _____

2. bath soap : cleanser : : aspirin : _____

3. eat : appetite : : behave : _____

4. collide : crash : : diminish : _____

5. caretaker : tend : : jailer : _____

3:3 Making Connections

The boldfaced words in the following sentences are short definitions of or synonyms for the five vocabulary words from the reading passage. On the line in front of each sentence, write the vocabulary word that has the same meaning as the boldfaced word or words.

remedy   eliminate   confined   disciplined   reduce

1. _____ Mary Ellen's cat did not scratch furniture or bite people because it had been **trained to behave properly** from the time it was a kitten.

2. _____ When baking brownies for a party, Gale decided to **leave out** the walnuts, because her friend Liz was allergic to them.

3. _____ The decision was made to print the school yearbook in black and white instead of in color, in order to **lower** the printing costs.

4. _____ Pamela was **unable to leave** the house for two weeks when she had pneumonia.

5. _____ Native Americans gave the colonists a simple **medicine** that they used to fight the fevers that were common in North America.

3:4 Making Connections

Complete each sentence with the correct vocabulary word.

remedy   eliminate   confined   disciplined   reduce

1. Reggie was _____ to his bedroom all evening as punishment for the fight he started with his brother.

2. A well-known _____ for hiccups is to breathe into a paper bag several times.

3. Mrs. Grossman _____ her students effectively without any yelling or threats.

4. A proposal to _____ the official number of school days from 180 to 165 was brought before the committee.

5. Carol decided to _____ ice cream, candy and baked goods from her diet in order to try to lose ten pounds.

4: The Roots of Our Language

dis-

The prefix *dis-* means not or the opposite of. We find it attached to the beginning of many English root words. Attached to *agree,* for instance, it gives us *disagree,* which means to not agree or to argue. And by affixing *dis-* to *comfort,* we get *discomfort,* meaning lack of comfort, or uneasiness. A disability, of course, is a lack of ability in some area.

You are probably also familiar with the words *discontinue* and *disapprove.* *Discontinue* means to stop doing something, which is the opposite of continuing, and *disapprove* means to not approve of something.

aster

Another word that begins with the prefix *dis-* is *disaster.* Though you probably know that a disaster is an event that causes great misfortune and suffering, you may well wonder what the *aster* part of the word means. Well, *aster* means star, and the word *disaster* came into being in the sixteenth century. At that time, many people believed in astrology, which is a kind of fortune-telling by studying the positions of the stars and planets. If the stars and planets were arranged in a way that was not considered lucky, any undesirable event that occurred at that time was called a disaster—a mishap due to the stars being arranged in an unlucky manner. So you can see why *disaster* means against the stars.

-logy

Notice that the word *astrology* also contains a form of *aster—astro.* The suffix *-logy* means study or science of. Though astrology was considered a science long ago, modern scientists do not take it seriously. The modern science of the stars and planets is called astronomy.

Have you ever worn a disguise to try to fool someone? If you have ever dressed up in a costume to go trick-or-treating on Halloween you have. A disguise is clothing worn to hide a person's true identity. If you disguise yourself, you are trying to fool people into believing you are someone else. *Guise* itself can mean costume or style of dress: *Harold went out into the night in the guise of a pirate.* It can also mean appearance: *She came in the guise of a friend, but then she was unkind to me.* So someone who is disguised does not have his or her regular appearance.

orient

If you are trying to find your way to an unfamiliar place, you may make a wrong turn and become disoriented—unable to figure out which way to go to correct your error. You might also become disoriented if you turn around fast several times and get dizzy. To be disoriented means to have lost your sense of direction or your sense of time or place. It means to be confused about where to go, where you are, or what's going on around you. The root word *orient* may mean either to arrange something in the proper way or to get one's bearings—figure out where one is and which direction to move in to go the right way. When traveling, people often orient themselves by studying a map and perhaps a compass. Chairs that are arranged for an audience in a hall are usually oriented, or faced, toward the stage.

lodge

Finally let's look at *dislodge.* If you are flying a kite on a windy day and the kite becomes lodged in a tree, you'd better cut your kite string and go home. Likewise, if you shoot an arrow into a target and it lodges there, you made a good shot. You have probably gathered that *lodge* means to get caught or to stay in place. To *dislodge,* therefore, naturally means to force out of place, or to get something unstuck. If you want to dislodge your kite from the tree, for instance, you may have to climb the tree.

Now let's discontinue this lesson and go on to some exercises.

4:1 Write each word or root listed on the left beside its meaning on the right.

dis-   1. _____ not or the opposite of

discontinue 2. _____ to stay in place

-logy   3. _____ to arrange in the proper way

orient   4. _____ the study or science of

lodge   5. _____ to stop doing

4:2 Mark each statement as either true or false.

_____ 1. A television series that has been discontinued permanently will be back on the air the next season.

_____ 2. A person who is disoriented knows exactly where he or she is.

_____ 3. A badminton birdie that is stuck in the net is lodged there.

_____ 4. The word *astrology* no longer means study of the stars, because astrology is no longer considered a legitimate science.

_____ 5. When two people feel, think and talk about something in exactly the same way, they are having a disagreement.

4:3 Answer the following questions.

1. If someone dislodges a bird nest, what have they done? _____

_____

2. To wear a disguise successfully, what must you change or hide? _____

_____

3. Sometimes when you are awakened suddenly, you experience a feeling of confusion—a loss of your sense of time and place. What word from the lesson describes what you are at that point?

_____

4. If you know that *dis-* means the opposite of, and that *ease* means freedom from pain or discomfort, what word can you make with those roots that means sickness, or experiencing pain and discomfort?

_____

5. You learned in the lesson that *-logy* means the study of. If *geo-* means the earth, what do you think geology is? _____

5: Extending Your Word Power

5:1 Multiple Meanings

Below are four vocabulary words that you met in this unit. Each word has more than one meaning. Use the words to fill in the blanks in the sentences that follow. In the sentences, the words have a meaning that is different from the meaning they had in the reading selections you read. If you are unsure of the various meanings of a word, look it up in the glossary.

disciplined   posture   reduced   originated

1. The snow was _____ to a slushy mess after a few hours of warm

   sunshine.

2. The ancient Romans, who ran hot-water pipes beneath their stone floors,

   _____ the idea of central heating.

3. In current events class, Mr. Valentino asked for opinions on the present

   _____ of the country in terms of foreign policy.

4. Leonard laughed so hard at the Marx Brothers movie that he was _____

   to tears.

5. Marie was severely _____ for getting home two hours past her curfew.

5:2 Roots Review

The incomplete sentences below contain words that you learned in the two roots lessons in this unit. Complete each sentence so that it makes sense and shows the meaning of the boldfaced vocabulary word.

1. When Tom **discontinued** his trumpet lessons _____

   _____ .

2. Sheila enjoys **astronomy** because _____

_____ .

3. The boys **adapted** the rules of the game so that _____

_____ .

4. So that he could sit **adjacent** to Charlie, Ted _____

_____ .

5. Jack became **disoriented** when _____

_____ .

6. To **orient** herself in the woods, Gretchen _____

_____ .

7. In the **guise** of a police officer, Max Crumble _____

_____ .

8. Because the stamp wouldn't **adhere**, _____

_____ .

9. Though Micky tried and tried to **dislodge** the stone, _____

_____ .

10. A record album was an **apt** gift for Laurie because _____

_____ .

5:3 Choosing Just the Right Word

As you have seen in the exercises in lessons one and three of this unit, many of the words you have worked with have a number of synonyms. In some cases the synonyms are slightly different in meaning. It is up to you to choose the words that express your ideas as strongly and clearly as possible.

In this exercise, synonym studies are provided for three of your vocabulary words. Use either the vocabulary words or their synonyms to complete the sentences in the exercise. Refer to the synonym studies as you decide which choice carries the best meaning for the specific context of each sentence. The word in the sentence may appear in a different tense than it does in the synonym study.

confine   limit

Confine and *limit* both mean to set bounds for. *Confine* suggests severe limitations—being kept or held in. *Marjorie was confined to her room for the evening because she had not done her chores. Jack is confined to a low-level job because of a lack of education. Limit* implies setting a point or line beyond which something cannot or is not allowed to go. A limit may be set in time, space, speed or degree. *The speed of the aircraft is limited by the power of its engines. The time limit on the test is twenty minutes.*

1. When Jeanne dances, she _____ her movements to the upper part of her body.

2. Mrs. Gantry asked Matthew to _____ his thoughts to issues of grammar while in English class, instead of daydreaming about other things.

3. While working on an assembly line in a candy factory, Ellen was _____ to a space about four feet square.

submissive   obedient

Submissive and *obedient* describe people who are doing what they've been told to do. A submissive person continually gives in to what other people want, while an obedient person simply follows rules set by authority.

4. In his large family, Benjamin found it easier to be _____ than to stand up for his own rights.

5. Most drivers are _____ and stop for red lights.

originate   begin

> *Originate* and *begin* both have to do with a starting point. To begin means to start or to do the first part of something. To originate means to come into existence or to be born. *The idea originated in a small laboratory in France.*

6. The play *Charles DeGaulle in France* _____ with a scene on a battlefield in Normandy.

7. The paper company _____ in San Francisco over forty years ago.

8. Marc wondered where the folktale about the boy and the elephant

_____ .

5:4 Recognizing Other Word Forms
The words below are other forms of the vocabulary words you have worked with in this unit. Fill in the blank in each sentence with the appropriate word. If you are unsure of the meaning of a word, look it up in the glossary.

origin   indication   submit   reduction

discipline   confines   remedied

1. The strict _____ within the Robinson household left little room for fun and games.

2. Tracy learned that she had to _____ to the coach's rules in order to remain on the track team.

3. Seeing Helen's fear of the dog, Jim _____ the situation by putting the animal in the house.

4. When Tracy heard of the tradition of buttering people's noses on their birthdays, she wondered what the _____ of the strange practice could have been.

5. In the _____ of his room, Marco could relax and forget about what other people expected of him.

6. The shoes were expensive, so Beverly waited two weeks for a further

_____ in the price before buying them.

7. The sharp, cold air provided a clear _____ that winter was just around the corner.

5:5 Putting Your Vocabulary to Use

Use vocabulary words from both this unit and the last one to complete the crossword puzzle.

ACROSS

2. involving two
4. obediently passive
6. uneasiness
7. get rid of
9. change to fit or to make work
11. confused about which direction to go in
12. group of fans
13. begin
15. consequence
16. custom

DOWN

1. does as told
3. double over on itself
4. give in
5. sign
8. sticky substance
10. great misfortune
14. reach

leasure or Punishment?

It is sometimes said that puns are the lowest form of humor, but that is only true of bad puns. A good pun is clever and holds the delightful element of surprise that is the foundation of all good jokes.

A pun is usually defined as "a play on words," but that definition isn't very satisfactory. Just what is a play on words? Well, of course puns are word jokes—the key words themselves are humorous in some way. But what makes them so? The basis of every pun is a word or a phrase that has a double meaning. In a truly good pun, both meanings make sense, and the mind goes back and forth between the two meanings. The effect is much like that created by the classic drawing that can be seen as either a vase or two heads facing each other, depending on how the viewer focuses on it.

William Shakespeare, a great wordsmith if ever there was one, could manufacture an admirable pun. In *Julius Caesar,* he presented a cobbler who says that he is "a mender of bad soles." The homonym of *soles—souls*—creates the pun. The same cobbler says that he meddles "with no tradesman's matters, nor women's matters, but with awl." Here the pun is on the word *awl.* An awl is a pointed tool used by a cobbler to make holes in leather, and its name is a homonym of *all,* meaning "everything."

Some less literary puns appear below. You can judge for yourself whether they are good or bad. If your reaction is a groan rather than a grin, you can be pretty sure that the pun is approaching the lower end of the humor scale.

Two ghosts drifted into a tavern and asked the bartender, "Do you serve spirits here?"

"If you can make a joke on any subject," roared the king to his jester, "try making one on me." "Ah," said the jester, "the king is not a subject."

When a group of miniature cattle were put in *Sputnik,* it became the herd shot round the world.

Once a hunter in the woods lost his dog, so he put an ear to a tree and listened to the bark.

The big firecracker said to the little firecracker, "My pop's bigger than your pop!"

"Don't tell me. You guys want to report another beating, right?"

UNIT 3

1: Meeting Words in Context

Reading Selection   The Birth of Aviation

Words Introduced   discontinuing devote conducted stern sprightly

2: The Roots of Our Language

Roots Introduced   un- il- ill- in- im- non-

3: Meeting Words in Context

Reading Selection   With the Greatest of Ease

Words Introduced   sustained formally shrewd fulfilled exceeded

4: The Roots of Our Language

Roots Introduced   ex- clu cava

5: Extending Your Word Power

Multiple Meanings
Roots Review
Using Words Precisely
Recognizing Other Word Forms
Putting Your Vocabulary to Use

1: Meeting Words in Context

The Birth of Aviation

Kitty Hawk and Kill Devil Hill are American place-names that will live in history. There Wilbur and Orville Wright made the world's first successful flight of a heavy, manned, power-driven machine.

On December 17, 1903, the machine was flown with a person on board for the first time. It was a cold and windy morning when Orville Wright climbed aboard the plane. His first power-driven flight, a distance of 120 feet, lasted just twelve seconds. From that achievement of the Wrights, the science of aeronautics developed.

Wilbur and Orville started out selling bicycles. They formed the Wright Cycle Company in 1892. Business was good, and they soon added a repair shop. The brothers twice moved their growing business to larger quarters. As a next step, they began to manufacture bicycles. Eventually they came up with a low-priced model known as the

Wright Special. They manufactured several hundred Wright Specials before **discontinuing** the business in order to **devote** full time to aviation.

Repairing and manufacturing bicycles sharpened the brothers' mechanical skills. In their construction of flying machines, Wilbur and Orville often used the same equipment and tools they used to repair bicycles. They **conducted** many experiments in the back room of their shop, and most of the parts used in the first successful airplane were built there.

Despite their devotion to hard work, Wilbur and Orville found time for the lighter side of life. They were not long-faced and **stern** but **sprightly** and good-humored. They loved small children and dogs, music and practical jokes. Close companions in their personal lives as well as in business, the brothers shared everything.

Choose from the story two words that are unfamiliar to you or whose meanings you are not completely sure of. (Do not choose words that appear in boldfaced type.) Write the words on the lines provided below. Then, beside each word, write what you think it means, based on how it was used in the story.

1. _____ : _____

   _____

2. _____ : _____

   _____

When you have finished the exercises in this lesson, go to your dictionary and find the definitions for the words you entered above. If a word has more than one meaning, look for the one that defines the word as it is used in the story. Then write the words and their dictionary definitions in the Student Words pages at the back of the book. How close did you come to figuring out their meanings for yourself?

1:1 Using Context

For each of the boldfaced words in this exercise, go back and read the sentence in which the word is used. Then, in the list that follows the vocabulary word, circle the words that have the same or almost the same meaning. Be prepared to give reasons for your choices.

1. **discontinuing** going on running stopping waiting ending closing

2. **devote** elect give sell fly divide apply

3. **conducted** did carried out played followed mixed led

4. **stern** happy serious kind impatient healthy unfriendly

5. **sprightly** slow old energetic religious happy beautiful

1:2 Making Connections

Listed below are the five vocabulary words from the reading passage. The list is followed by definitions of the words as they are used in the passage. Write each word in front of its definition.

discontinue   devote   conducted   stern   sprightly

1. _____ : performed, carried on

2. _____ : put an end to

3. _____ : severe, harsh

4. _____ : lively, spirited

5. _____ : give full attention to

1:3 Making Connections

Complete the following analogies by inserting one of the five vocabulary words in the blank at the end of each one. Remember that in an analogy the last two words or phrases must be related to each other in the same way that the first two are related. The colon in an analogy is read "is to," and the symbol : : is read "as." So "high : low : : wide : narrow" is read "high is to low as wide is to narrow."

discontinue   devote   conduct   stern   sprightly

1. write : print : : stop : _____

2. happy : funny : : serious : _____

3. runner : fast : : elf : _____

4. cake : bake : : experiment : _____

5. detest : adore : : neglect : _____

1:4 Making Connections

Complete each sentence with the correct vocabulary word.

discontinuing   devote   conducted   stern   sprightly

1. To help visitors learn about the wonders of the pine forest, the park offers nature walks _____ by trained guides.

2. Though he just celebrated his ninetieth birthday, Mr. Borden remains unusually alert and _____ .

3. After failing math, John promised his parents he would _____ more time and energy to his studies.

4. Mrs. Joel's _____ face, with her tight lips and disapproving eyes, told Henry that she was not pleased to find him digging for worms in her front yard.

5. The bookstore has a policy of _____ any book that sells fewer than two copies a year.

2: The Roots of Our Language

un-

Undoubtedly you already understand and use many words that contain the prefix *un-*, which means not or the opposite of. It is a common and highly useful prefix, for it provides an easy way to express the opposite of a positive word. *Happy* becomes *unhappy, fair* becomes *unfair,* and *even* becomes *uneven.* And if you know the meanings of a root word, it is easy to figure out the meaning of the same word with the prefix *un-* attached to it. One meaning of *civilized,* for example, is "showing culture and good manners—refined." Clearly then, someone who goes to school with hair in tangles, sits on the floor in the classroom and speaks with a mouth full of food might be justly said to be uncivilized.

il-
ill-

Un- is not the only prefix that means not. *Il-* and *ill-* also have that meaning. *Illegal* means not legal, and *illogical* means not logical—not reasonable or correctly thought out, for logic is reasoned thought. Do you know what *illiterate* means? If you know that *literate* means able to read and write, then it's easy to figure out. *Illiterate* is just the opposite. Illiteracy, then, is the lack of knowledge of how to read and write. When you hear or read in the news that there is a high rate of illiteracy, it means that there are many people who do not know how to read and write. *Legible* means plain and clear—easy to read. It is used to refer to handwriting. A person with legible handwriting writes clearly. If you were to get a letter from a friend whose handwriting was illegible, you would not be able to figure out what the letter said. It is illadvised (not advised, or advised against) that you do your homework assignments so quickly and carelessly that they are illegible, for your teacher may become illhumored (not in a good humor, or in a bad mood) and make you do the work over again.

in-

Still another way of expressing the opposite of a root word is with the prefix *in-. Incorrect,* therefore, means not correct, and *incapable* means not capable, or not able. If you can't do something no matter how hard you try, you may have an inability—lack of ability—to do that thing.

You must be careful with the prefix *in-*, because it can also mean inside. *Indoors* and *inhabited,* for instance, do not mean not doors and not inhabited. *Indoors* means inside a building, and *inhabited* means lived in. A house that is inhabited is one in which people live.

im-

A prefix with a meaning similar to that of *in-* is *im-. Im-* means not in such words as *impossible* (not possible), *improper* (not proper), and *immobile* (not mobile—not able to move, or not able to be moved). Also like *in-*, *im-* can mean in. An import, for instance, is an object that is brought in, usually from a foreign place. Likewise, when people are imprisoned, they are put in prison.

non-

Finally, there is one other negative prefix. *Non-* can mean not, the opposite of, or the lack of. Nonsense is talk or action that does not make sense, meaning that it is foolish or silly. A nonprofit organization does not make a profit, which means that it does not seek to take in more money than the amount needed to run the organization. Someone who believes in nonviolence believes in using peaceful methods to solve problems. He or she is against violence of any kind.

There we have it—the prefixes that usually mean not or the opposite of: *un, il* and *ill, in-, im-* and *non-.* The meanings of words that carry those prefixes are usually the opposite of the meanings of the root words alone.

2:1 Write each word or root listed on the left beside its meaning on the right.

in-   1. _____ not able to move

immobile   2. _____ not able

nonsense   3. _____ not readable

incapable   4. _____ not

illegible   5. _____ talk or action that makes no sense

2:2 Mark each statement as either true or false.

_____ 1. An illegible contract is not legal.

_____ 2. An inhabited building has people living in it.

_____ 3. Someone with a broken leg is incapable of dancing.

_____ 4. Ships are often used to carry imports to other countries.

_____ 5. The best readers are illiterate.

2:3 Put an *x* in front of the answer choice you think is correct.

1. A request that comes at a bad time is

   ☐ a. untimed.   ☐ b. timely.   ☐ c. ill-timed.

2. Someone who is angry is

   ☐ a. humorous.   ☐ b. ill-humored.   ☐ c. inhuman.

3. Driving faster than the speed limit is

   ☐ a. illegal.   ☐ b. illegible.   ☐ c. illogical.

4. Foreign goods that are sold in this country are

   ☐ a. important.   ☐ b. improper.   ☐ c. imported.

5. The convicted criminal was immediately

   ☐ a. imposed.   ☐ b. improved.   ☐ c. imprisoned.

3: Meeting Words in Context

With the Greatest of Ease

Orville Wright made his first public flight on September 3, 1908, at Fort Myer, Virginia. He was testing an airplane for possible use by the U.S. government. He circled the field one and a half times on the first test. Theodore Roosevelt, Jr., is reported to have said, "When the plane first rose, the crowd's gasp of surprise was not alone at the wonder of it, but because it was so unexpected." Orville's last flight at Fort Myer in 1908 ended in tragedy. The airplane crashed, killing Lt. Thomas Selfridge, a passenger. Orville himself **sustained** broken ribs, a fractured leg, and hip injuries.

In 1909, Orville completed the government test flights by flying just under forty-three miles an hour. The United States Army **formally** accepted its first airplane from the Wrights on August 2, 1909. During the same year, the brothers enjoyed further flying triumphs both in Europe and at home. While Orville was making great flights in Germany, Wilbur was doing the same in New York.

The brothers established their first airplane manufacturing companies in France and Germany. Later the Wright Company was organized in the United States as well, with Wilbur as president and Orville as vice president. In financial affairs the Wrights were surprisingly **shrewd**. But though they became wealthy and famous, they did not feel **fulfilled** as businessmen. They looked forward to the time when they could retire and spend their days doing scientific research.

Orville returned to Kill Devil Hill in October 1911 to experiment with an automatic control device and to make soaring flights with a glider. On October 24 he set a new world record for soaring, which was not **exceeded** until ten years later. On May 30, 1912, Wilbur Wright died of typhoid fever at the age of forty-five. Orville outlived him by thirty-six years.

Choose from the story two words that are unfamiliar to you or whose meanings you are not completely sure of. (Do not choose words that appear in boldfaced type.) Write the words on the lines provided below. Then, beside each word, write what you think it means, based on how it was used in the story.

1. _____ : _____

   _____

2. _____ : _____

When you have finished the exercises in this lesson, go to your dictionary and find the definitions for the words you entered above. If a word has more than one meaning, look for the one that defines the word as it is used in the story. Then write the words and their dictionary definitions in the Student Words pages at the back of the book. How close did you come to figuring out their meanings for yourself?

3:1 Using Context

Below are five sentences from the reading passage. From the four answer choices that follow each sentence, choose the one that gives the best definition of the boldfaced word. Put an *x* in the box beside it. Use the context, or setting, provided by the sentence to help you discover the meaning of the word. If the sentence itself does not provide enough clues, go back to the passage and read the paragraph in which the sentence appears.

1. Orville himself **sustained** broken ribs, a fractured leg, and hip injuries.
   - ☐ a. got away with
   - ☐ b. experienced
   - ☐ c. hated
   - ☐ d. caused

2. The United States Army **formally** accepted its first airplane from the Wrights on August 2, 1909.
   - ☐ a. later
   - ☐ b. happily
   - ☐ c. officially
   - ☐ d. finally

3. In financial affairs the Wrights were surprisingly **shrewd**.
   - ☐ a. sharp minded
   - ☐ b. lazy
   - ☐ c. stupid
   - ☐ d. innocent

4. But though they became wealthy and famous, they did not feel **fulfilled** as businessmen.
   - ☐ a. excited
   - ☐ b. capable
   - ☐ c. satisfied
   - ☐ d. respected

5. On October 24 he set a new world record for soaring, which was not **exceeded** until ten years later.
   - ☐ a. topped
   - ☐ b. recorded
   - ☐ c. noticed
   - ☐ d. lowered

3:2 Making Connections

Listed below are the five vocabulary words from the reading passage, followed by fourteen words and phrases that are related to them in some way. They may be synonyms, antonyms or definitions. On the line next to each word or phrase, write the vocabulary word that is related to it.

sustained   formally   shrewd   fulfilled   exceeded

1. intelligent _____

2. dissatisfied _____

3. surpassed _____

4. underwent _____

5. with ceremony _____

6. suffered _____

7. outdid _____

8. dull _____

9. casually _____

10. went beyond _____

11. complete _____

12. escaped _____

13. clever _____

14. legally _____

3:3 Making Connections

The boldfaced words in the following sentences are short definitions of or synonyms for the five vocabulary words from the reading passage. On the line in front of each sentence, write the vocabulary word that has the same meaning as the boldfaced word or words.

sustained   **formally**   **shrewd**   **fulfilled**   **exceeded**

1. _____ The **keenly perceptive** observations that Nina expressed in her answer to the essay question greatly impressed her teacher.

2. _____ In the track meet, Donald **surpassed** the previous high school record for the forty-yard dash.

3. _____ The car was totalled in the crash, and Janet **suffered** a bruised arm and a bad gash on the forehead.

4. _____ Mr. Warner did not dislike his job as program director of Channel 12, but he did not feel **completely satisfied** in his work, either.

5. _____ There were many rumors about the outcome of the student council election, but the winners had not yet been **officially** announced.

3:4 Making Connections

Complete each sentence with the correct vocabulary word.

sustained   **formally**   **shrewd**   **fulfilled**   **exceeded**

1. Lisa and John see each other in the hallway every day, but they have never been

_____ introduced.

2. The cost of the house repairs _____ the Robinson's budget by several

hundred dollars.

3. Is it possible for a woman to be _____ as a mother and homemaker?

4. Clifford _____ a great loss when his dog, a lovable fox terrier, was

killed by a car.

5. After careful research, the bankers made a _____ decision to raise

interest rates.

4: The Roots of Our Language

ex-

The prefix *ex-*, meaning out of, from or former, appears affixed to many English words. It usually holds the meaning of former when it is attached to the names of occupations, such as in *expresident, exbaseball star* and *exsailor*. You can add *ex-* to nearly any occupation to mean someone who formerly had a certain position or job.

In many words, *ex-* carries its "out of" meaning. The word *exclude*, for example, means to shut out or keep out. The related word *exclusive* means not shared with others. It can also mean excluding others. When a magazine gets an exclusive on a news story, it means that no other magazine can carry the story. A club whose membership is open only to certain types or groups of people is said to be exclusive.

clu

The *clu* in *exclude* and *exclusive* comes from the Latin root meaning close or shut. So those words mean, literally, to shut out. The word *closet* comes from a closely related root meaning enclosure. A closet is a closed room for storing things. *Closet* may also be a verb, meaning to shut oneself off in a room by oneself.

cava

Ex- also appears in *excavate*. To excavate is to dig out, to dig a hole, or to hollow something out. The *cava* part of the word comes from Greek and Latin words meaning hollow. Thus, a cave is a hollow chamber in the ground. A hollow, of course, is formed when something is removed: *The workers excavated the side of the mountain to make the tunnel. Excavate* can also mean to expose by digging away a covering. Archaeologists, for instance, excavate the sites of ancient civilizations. The place where they excavate is called an excavation. Excavation is also the act of excavating: *The excavation of the site was moving along smoothly.*

Ex- can be found paired with two root words related to breath: *exhale* and *expire*. *Exhale* means to breathe out. It is the opposite of *inhale*, which means to breathe in. *Expire* can also mean to breathe out, but its more common meanings are to come to an end, and to die. You have probably heard the expression "to breathe one's last breath," meaning to die. A person who is dead can be said to have expired. Also, things that are issued for a set period of time, such as library cards and driver's licenses, expire at the end of the period for which they are issued. They become invalid—no longer usable. The word *spirit* also grew from the Latin root for breathe. Thus, *expire* with the meaning of dying also means to let the spirit out. *Inspire*, which means to move or guide by supernatural means, or to spur on, came from roots meaning to take in the spirit. It is also a synonym for *inhale*.

If all this has left you breathless, perhaps we should look at one more *ex-* word, *explode*, meaning to burst apart with a loud noise, or to blow up. This word had an interesting beginning. It came from the Latin word *explodere*, which meant to drive off the stage by clapping. The first English meaning of *explode* was to drive from the stage by noisy disapproval. Today, of course, we clap to show *approval* of a stage performance. When we use *explode* to refer to the violent demolition of a building, we mean that the building blew out, or apart, due to great pressure from within. In many crowded cities today, buildings that need to be taken down are *im*ploded. To implode means to burst inward. When a huge building implodes, it does not blow apart. Rather, it falls in on itself, thereby leaving nearby buildings undamaged.

4:1 Write each word or root listed on the left beside its meaning on the right.

expire   1. _____ to close or shut out

exclusive   2. _____ former

exclude   3. _____ hollow

cava   4. _____ not shared with others

ex-   5. _____ to end, die

4:2 Mark each statement as either true or false.

_____ 1. An exclusive interview will be published in newspapers everywhere.

_____ 2. To excavate means to shut someone out.

_____ 3. When a building implodes fragments are scattered for great distances.

_____ 4. An expilot no longer commands an aircraft.

_____ 5. Dinosaur bones and fossils might be found in an excavation.

4:3 Complete the following sentences.

1. Shortly after we inhale, we _____ .

2. An area in which a large pit has been dug has been _____ .

3. An organization to which only businessmen can belong is _____ .

4. A library card that is no longer good has _____ .

5. The opposite of interior is _____ .

5: Extending Your Word Power

5:1 Multiple Meanings

Below are five vocabulary words that you met in this unit. Each has more than one meaning. Use the words to fill in the blanks in the sentences that follow. In those sentences, the words have a meaning that is different from the meaning they had in the stories you read. If you are unsure of the various meanings of a word, look up the word in the glossary.

fulfilled   conducted   devote   sustain   formally

1. The architects were asked to design a small bridge that could _____ the equivalent weight of eight grown elephants.

2. Electricity is normally _____ by means of wires running from the source of power to the electrical appliance.

3. As best man at his brother's wedding, Jim had to dress _____ , in a tuxedo.

4. Some people feel such a strong desire to see all the countries of the world working together that they _____ themselves completely to the cause of world peace.

5. After years of hard work, Alicia finally _____ her lifelong dream of a travel adventure by setting off on a trip around the world.

5:2 Roots Review

The incomplete sentences below contain words that you learned in the two roots lessons in this unit. Complete each sentence so that it makes sense and shows the meaning of the boldfaced vocabulary word.

1. The letter was so **illegible** that _____

_____ .

2. Because Sophie believed in **nonviolence**, she _____
_____ .

3. On Saturday Henry went to see the **excavation** of _____
_____ .

4. When making potato salad, Jim **excludes** onions because _____
_____ .

5. Since she is **incapable** of getting to the dance, Beth _____
_____ .

6. Because he is **illiterate**, Sam decided to _____
_____ .

7. When the big old hotel **imploded**, it _____
_____ .

8. Because the coupon had **expired**, _____
_____ .

9. When CBS got **exclusive** rights to televise the Olympics, _____
_____ .

10. The boy became **immobile** when _____
_____ .

5:3 Choosing Just the Right Word

Many of the words you have worked with in this unit have a number of synonyms. As you know, in some cases the synonyms have different shades of meaning.

Following are synonym studies for two of your vocabulary words. Use either the vocabulary words or their synonyms to complete the sentences in the exercise that follows. Refer to the synonym studies as you decide which choice carries the best meaning for the specific context of each sentence.

discontinue   pause

> *Discontinue* and *pause* both mean to stop an action. *Discontinue,* however, is used when speaking of the permanent stopping of a regular activity or practice. *Tom discontinued his piano lessons because he didn't have enough time to practice. Pause* means to stop for a short time. *Cindy paused in her walk to pick some flowers.*

1. Carol decided to _____ her subscription to the news magazine.

2. When there was a _____ in the conversation, Danny told his joke.

intelligent   shrewd   clever

> *Intelligent, shrewd* and *clever* all mean mentally sharp or quick. *Intelligent* is usually used when speaking of someone's ability to do well in new situations or to solve problems. *It is clear from the fact that Robert can look at any machine and figure out how it works that he is very intelligent. Clever* suggests a natural quickness or skill in doing a particular thing. *Roger is very clever at making up puns. Shrewd* suggests cleverness and craftiness in practical things. It often implies mischievousness and meanness. *Max shrewdly asked for more money than the car was worth, knowing that customers like to dicker.*

3. It is obvious from the way Mindy talks other people into doing her work for her that she is

   quite _____ .

4. Tony is very _____ when it comes to writing vocabulary sentences in

   class.

5. Frieda was _____ enough to teach herself computer programming.

5:4 Recognizing Word Forms

The words listed below are other forms of the vocabulary words you have worked with in this unit. Fill in the blank in each sentence with the appropriate word. Use what you have learned about the vocabulary in the unit to help you figure out what these words mean. If you need more help, refer to the glossary.

formalized   conductor   excess   devotion   fulfillment   sustenance

1. So many people volunteered to clean up the neighborhood that there was actually an

   _____ of help for the project.

2. Pablo's mother packed a lunch of peanut butter sandwiches and fruit for

_____ on the long train trip.

3. In January Ted and Mary Jane decided to marry, but their engagement was not

_____ until early March.

4. For Andrea, becoming a doctor was the _____ of a lifelong dream.

5. A solar panel serves as a _____ of heat and energy from the sun.

6. In the Orient, _____ to one's elders is an important element of

family life.

5:5 Putting Your Vocabulary to Use

The word-search puzzle on the following page contains fifteen vocabulary words from units two and three. They are printed horizontally, vertically, diagonally, backward and upside down.

Begin by listing the vocabulary words next to their clues below. Then find the words in the puzzle, circling them as you locate them.

1. _____ cure

2. _____ put an end to an activity

3. _____ against the law

4. _____ imprisoned

5. _____ having no manners; uncultured

6. _____ body position

7. _____ serious, harsh

8. _____ the giving of great care and attention to something

9. _____ to shut or keep out

10. _____ to change appearance in order to hide one's identity

11. _____ not for purposes of making money

12. _____ lively and spirited

13. _____ next to

14. _____ uncover by digging

15. _____ performed; carried out

```
b  c  e  i  v  b  a  u  n  c  i  v  i  l  i  z  e  d  t  b  d
i  p  h  l  n  n  e  o  c  o  i  o  a  d  v  b  i  i  c  w  o
e  f  i  v  o  g  p  d  e  n  a  d  e  b  c  i  p  q  l  e  u
g  e  o  c  i  t  g  s  r  d  q  e  i  i  o  b  i  x  o  b  p
e  r  o  p  b  m  m  n  e  u  n  i  t  n  o  c  s  i  d  o  w
g  i  v  o  b  m  d  g  s  c  o  e  g  i  a  s  i  p  o  s  t
h  f  r  w  p  i  o  r  e  t  i  o  p  g  h  k  o  i  p  s  e
t  r  e  i  p  h  l  g  m  e  t  r  e  s  r  t  p  r  g  h  l
r  o  n  o  i  t  o  v  e  d  d  r  i  o  p  i  i  o  p  r  t
p  o  o  i  l  p  o  v  e  d  o  i  w  a  g  g  d  g  p  l  n
t  r  n  o  e  a  i  o  n  m  g  e  o  i  h  e  t  r  e  p  t
w  r  p  o  i  o  g  i  e  g  o  h  v  t  o  i  e  t  o  p  b
o  t  r  i  o  n  g  e  i  e  g  v  l  e  r  t  a  p  t  l  n
t  y  o  a  s  f  x  i  l  o  t  y  r  d  p  v  e  r  p  u  l
e  t  f  o  j  c  o  l  g  l  y  r  t  a  a  w  y  r  n  h  d
d  t  i  p  l  s  d  v  j  k  i  y  g  c  n  b  c  r  d  k  h
h  g  t  u  e  d  s  u  p  l  g  m  x  d  s  g  v  n  i  g  r
f  t  d  h  b  n  p  l  m  h  u  e  a  e  s  d  c  g  s  g  e
s  e  v  b  o  p  l  m  s  t  e  r  n  i  n  g  e  d  g  o  m
w  r  d  t  h  g  p  l  u  m  n  v  g  d  t  e  r  s  u  t  e
a  s  d  r  w  h  g  u  p  l  m  f  n  h  t  y  e  d  i  t  d
p  d  e  n  i  f  n  o  c  i  t  d  a  v  b  p  k  l  s  r  y
w  r  t  p  l  h  m  f  t  e  v  d  t  r  w  p  l  g  e  t  v
h  b  t  d  r  e  w  p  l  n  j  s  r  t  b  d  v  p  l  y  h
e  t  g  d  b  v  c  p  l  a  y  o  p  o  s  t  u  r  e  h  g
d  c  u  p  l  h  m  b  c  y  p  k  g  j  b  u  t  r  s  r  w
a  r  t  p  l  g  m  e  s  t  e  h  b  n  f  m  p  l  e  r  w
p  l  h  m  r  t  n  e  t  h  m  f  b  c  e  p  l  y  r  n  d
a  r  v  e  y  t  n  e  b  v  g  t  p  l  u  h  m  t  r  e  w
```

ictionary

What is the meaning of this? That's just the question that forms the basis of the game of Fictionary. No need to be a whiz at words to enjoy it. The main requirements are imagination and a sense of humor. You'll also need a dictionary, some pencils and paper, and at least three people (but the more the better!).

In Fictionary, you are asked to make up definitions for words that you don't know the real meaning of. The definitions should sound as much like real dictionary definitions as possible, because the object of the game is to fool the other players into believing that your definition is the true one—that's where the "fiction" part of the game's name comes from. The fictitious definitions can get pretty absurd, and sometimes hilarious, but then some of the real definitions turn out to be awfully strange too.

Intrigued? Here are the rules:

(1) Give each person some slips of paper or several index cards, and a pen or pencil. Players should write their names on their cards. Each person plays for himself or herself—there are no teams.

(2) Choose one person to be the leader of the first round. (After the first round, each person in the group should take a turn being the leader.) The leader picks a word from the dictionary. Any word may be chosen, but it should be a word that no one knows the meaning of. If any player knows the word, he or she must say so, and a different word must be picked. (You might want to try to choose a word that has a particularly funny or strange meaning.) The leader should say the word and spell it for the other players.

(3) Every player, including the leader, should write a definition for the word. (Of course the leader knows the real definition, but he or she still gets a chance to try to fool the others.) You should try to write as crafty and real-sounding a definition as you can. The leader should also write the real definition on a card.

(4) When everyone has written a definition, the leader collects the cards and numbers them. The numbers are used instead of the players' names to identify the definitions. That way no one knows who wrote which definition. The leader reads all the definitions out loud, including the real definition, identifying each by number. For example, "Definition number 3, *mollify:* to launch into the air at such an angle that the force of gravity has very little effect, thereby allowing the object to float for a period of time."

(5) Every player votes out loud, by number, for the definition he or she thinks is correct. The leader tallies the votes for each definition.

(6) Points are scored in two ways. First, anyone who votes for the correct definition gets a point. Second, a player gets a point for each vote his or her definition collects.

Play continues until time runs out or until a set number of of points is reached. The player with the most points wins.

"paprika noun. a small fur-bearing animal having unusually long claws, known for its high altitude nesting."

1: Meeting Words in Context

Reading Selection Where Lincoln Lived

Words Introduced fixed effects mere restored interlude

2: The Roots of Our Language

Roots Introduced de- duc tec

3: Meeting Words in Context

Reading Selection America's Sixteenth President

Words Introduced issued trying humble abundance
adopted

4: The Roots of Our Language

Roots Introduced re- ply cedere pre- -ject

5: Extending Your Word Power

Multiple Meanings
Roots Review
Using Words Precisely
Recognizing Other Word Forms
Putting Your Vocabulary to Use

1: Meeting Words in Context

Where Lincoln Lived

For the first thirty-five years of his life, Abraham Lincoln seemed to be always on the move. A log-cabin boy and frontiersman, he later wrote of himself as "a piece of floating driftwood." His boyhood homes were scattered across several states: Kentucky, Indiana and Illinois. At twenty-one he became a clerk at a store in New Salem, Illinois, at night stretching out his large frame on piles of straw in the back room. Even after he started practicing law he had no **fixed** home, but followed his cases from one small town to another.

When Springfield was named the state capital of Illinois, Lincoln thought the time had come to settle down. He rode into Springfield on a borrowed horse, with all his personal **effects** on his back and in his saddlebags.

Lincoln married Mary Todd in 1842. The first years of their life together were spent in boarding houses and at the Globe Tavern. After the birth of their son Robert, they bought a cottage on the corner of Eighth and Jackson Streets. The only home Lincoln ever owned cost a **mere** $1,500. He and his family lived there until he was elected president in 1861.

Lincoln had planned to go back to Springfield and to the house at Eighth and Jackson when his term in Washington was up. The presidency, he always said, was only an **interlude**. So he rented the house to a friend and told Billy Herndon, his law partner, to leave their office sign untouched. "If I live, I'm coming back, and we'll go right on practicing law as if nothing ever happened." But Lincoln never did return, for he was assassinated while in office.

Lincoln's Springfield home has been **restored**. Visitors can view the parlor with its plush-covered chairs and floral rugs. They can stand awhile by the four-poster bed in which Lincoln rested after straining his eyes over legal papers in flickering lamplight. They can wander through the sitting room where Mary sewed and Lincoln rocked with young son Tad on his knee. The true heart of Lincoln's memory beats in this simple house.

Choose from the story two words that are unfamiliar to you or whose meanings you are not completely sure of. (Do not choose words that appear in boldfaced type.) Write the words on the lines provided below. Then, beside each word, write what you think it means, based on how it was used in the story.

1. _____ : _____

   _____

2. _____ : _____

   _____

When you have finished the exercises in this lesson, go to your dictionary and find the definitions for the words you entered above. If a word has more than one meaning, look for the one that defines the word as it is used in the story. Then write the words and their dictionary definitions in the Student Words pages at the back of the book. How close did you come to figuring out their meanings for yourself?

1:1 Using Context

Put an *x* in the box beside each correct answer. For clues to the meanings of the words, reread the parts of the passage in which they appear.

1. In the passage, a **fixed** home is one that
   - ☐ a. is in good repair.
   - ☐ b. is always in the same place.
   - ☐ c. has been decorated by someone else.
   - ☐ d. costs a lot of money.

2. In the story, Lincoln's **effects** refer to his
   - ☐ a. habits.
   - ☐ c. belongings.
   - ☐ b. riding gear.
   - ☐ d. attitudes.

3. A **mere** $1,500 means
   - ☐ a. only that small amount.
   - ☐ b. approximately $1,500.
   - ☐ c. an enormous sum.
   - ☐ d. stolen money.

4. A **restored** home is one that has been
   - ☐ a. modernized.
   - ☐ b. returned to its original condition.
   - ☐ c. made into a store.
   - ☐ d. rebuilt for storage.

5. When Lincoln said the presidency was only an **interlude,** he meant that it
   - ☐ a. was just a job.
   - ☐ b. didn't pay enough for him to live on.
   - ☐ c. took him too far from his home.
   - ☐ d. was a temporary break from his lifework as a lawyer.

1:2 Making Connections

In this exercise, the list of vocabulary words is followed by definitions of the words as they are used in the story. Write each word in front of its definition.

fixed   effects   mere   restored   interlude

1. _____ : uncomplicated; that and no more

2. _____ : stationary; remaining in one place

3. _____ : a short period in between

4. _____ : repaired; returned to its original condition

5. _____ : personal property; belongings

1:3 Making Connections

Listed below are the five vocabulary words from the reading passage, followed by fourteen words and phrases that are related to them in some way. They may be synonyms, antonyms or definitions. On the line next to each word or phrase, write the vocabulary word that is related to it.

fixed   effects   mere   restored   interlude

1. simple _____

2. stationary _____

3. destroyed _____

4. main event _____

5. tremendous _____

6. personal property _____

7. small _____

8. time in between _____

9. space _____

10. bare _____

11. belongings _____

12. anchored in place _____

13. movable _____

14. fixed up _____

1:4 Making Connections

Complete each sentence with the correct vocabulary word.

fixed   effects   mere   restored   interlude

1. Jose was pleased to see so many old buildings in his neighborhood

_____ to bring out their nineteenth-century charm.

2. On their _____ income, the elderly couple could not afford many

treats after paying their regular bills.

3. Sarah, a _____ country girl, had a hard time adjusting to the

sophistication of her new city friends.

4. After a brief _____ of light-hearted joking, the mayor returned to the

serious business at hand.

5. The wealthy young man traveled with a butler who took care of his employer's personal

_____ .

2: The Roots of Our Language

de- The prefix *de-* has a number of meanings, all having to do with undoing. It may mean remove, the reverse of, reduce, get off, or do the opposite of.

A *de-* word that you will be familiar with if you have a bicycle with a number of sprocket wheels, or gear wheels (such as a ten-speed bike), is *derailleur* (dih-RAY-ler). A derailleur is a spring-loaded mechanism that changes the gears by causing the chain to move from one sprocket wheel to another. Its name comes from a French word with the same spelling that means "to throw off the track." When a train is derailed, it is thrown off the track, or rail. When a bicycle chain is derailed, it is taken off one sprocket wheel and put on another.

To *decode* means to take out of code. When a coded message is decoded, it is put into English, so it can be easily read. *Decompose* means the opposite of *compose*. *Compose* means to put together, to make up, or to form. Someone who invents new pieces of music—songs, symphonies, operas—is a composer. He or she composes music. A cake is composed of all its ingredients, and an organization is composed of all its members. Living organisms are composed of all their various kinds of molecules. So when we talk of living matter decomposing, we mean that it is rotting, or being separated into its basic elements, or ingredients. People who raise vegetables often throw all their vegetable matter—leaves, peelings, seeds—into a pile outside and wait for it to decompose, because the rotted matter makes a wonderful natural fertilizer for their gardens.

To *deduct* means to take away. For example, when you subtract, you deduct the subtrahend from the minuend to get the dividend. Workers often complain about all the deductions from their paychecks. In this case, a deduction is an amount taken away from the total earned. Deductions are often taken from earnings by an employer to pay a worker's social security benefits, income taxes and such. The more deductions, the less money the **duc** worker gets to take home. The *duc* part of *deductions* comes from the Latin *ducere,* meaning to lead. So deduct means, literally, to lead away or take away.

Ducere is also the basis for another word with the prefix *de-. Deduce* means to infer, or to arrive at a conclusion through putting facts and observations together. If a tea kettle is whistling, you can deduce that the water inside is boiling. You are led from the facts to the conclusion. So *de* plus *duce* means to lead from. The noun form of *deduce* is the same as the noun form of *deduct: deduction.* You make a deduction when you form an inference or draw a conclusion.

The root *ducere* is also the basis for the word *education.* With the addition of an *e* at the beginning, we have the Latin *educere,* meaning to lead forth. Education, of course, is a leading forth into knowledge. The *tion* on the end of the word is an English noun suffix. It tells us that *education* is a noun.

To go back to *deduction* once more, we should mention a person whose job it is to make deductions: the detective. It is a detective's job to make **tec** deductions from things he or she detects. The *tec* in *detect* and *detective* comes from a Latin root meaning to cover. So to detect is to uncover, or to find something that is hidden. When trying to solve criminal cases, detectives have to uncover hidden facts.

2:1   Write each word or root listed on the left beside its meaning on the right.

duc

detect

deduce

decompose

de-

1. _____ to rot

2. _____ to arrive at a conclusion

3. _____ to lead

4. _____ remove, reduce, the opposite of

5. _____ to find something hidden

2:2   Mark each statement as either true or false.

_____ 1. To read a coded message you must decode it.

_____ 2. All bicycles have derailleurs.

_____ 3. When matter separates into its basic elements, it decomposes.

_____ 4. Deduction is the leading forth into knowledge.

_____ 5. Many deductions make a paycheck larger.

2:3   Put an *x* in front of the answer choice you think is correct.

1. A successful detective often makes clever

   ☐ a. deceptions.   ☐ b. reductions.   ☐ c. deductions.

2. Vegetable matter left in a pile will

   ☐ a. decompress.   ☐ b. deduce.   ☐ c. decompose.

3. If a teacher deducts points from your grade on a test, you get

   ☐ a. a higher   ☐ b. a lower   ☐ c. a passing
         grade.   grade.   grade.

4. If the derailleur on your bicycle breaks, you cannot

   ☐ a. switch gears.   ☐ b. stop.   ☐ c. pedal.

5. A decomposed banana is

   ☐ a. unripe.   ☐ b. ripe.   ☐ c. rotten.

3: Meeting Words in Context

America's Sixteenth President

The Lincoln cent was first **issued** in 1909, to celebrate the 100th anniversary of the birth of Abraham Lincoln, sixteenth president of the United States. One side of the coin bears the profile of Lincoln as he looked during the **trying** years of the War Between the States. At that time, faced with the great problems of a divided nation, Lincoln worked hard to prevent the split between North and South. "A house divided against itself cannot stand," he warned the nation.

The reverse side of the Lincoln cent, from 1909 through 1958, had a simple design of two wheat heads (tops of the stalks, which hold the kernels). Wheat stands for **abundance**, which America offers its people not only in material wealth but also in the freedoms and liberties granted by the Constitution.

In 1959, to celebrate the 150th anniversary of Lincoln's birth, a new design was **adopted** for the back of the penny. Created by mint engraver Frank Gasparro, the design featured the Lincoln Memorial in Washington, D.C. Since the memorial is an outstanding tribute to the late president, it was a good choice.

Two years after Lincoln's death, plans were begun to build a monument to honor him. It was finally decided that a fitting memorial be erected in the national's capital, at the end of a long mall. Inside the building, a huge statue of Lincoln sitting in a chair symbolizes the greatness of the former president.

Lincoln was a man of **humble** birth. He was born in a log cabin in Kentucky, and as a boy he studied his lessons by candlelight. He enjoyed few of life's material comforts. Yet, through hard work, he rose to become the president of a nation, at one of the most difficult times in its history.

Choose from the story two words that are unfamiliar to you or whose meanings you are not completely sure of. (Do not choose words that appear in boldfaced type.) Write the words on the lines provided below. Then, beside each word, write what you think it means, based on how it was used in the story.

1. _____ : _____

   _____

2. _____ : _____

   _____

When you have finished the exercises in this lesson, go to your dictionary and find the definitions for the words you entered above. If a word has more than one meaning, look for the one that defines the word as it is used in the story. Then write the words and their dictionary definitions in the Student Words pages at the back of the book. How close did you come to figuring out their meanings for yourself?

3:1 Using Context

Write each vocabulary word beside its correct meaning. Try to figure out what the word means from the way it is used in the story.

1. **issued**

_____ given away   _____ put into circulation

_____ taken seriously   _____ spent

2. **trying**

_____ violent   _____ unusual

_____ suitable   _____ difficult

3. **humble**

_____ modest   _____ foreign

_____ noble   _____ significant

4. **abundance**

_____ freedom   _____ opportunity

_____ packages   _____ plenty

5. **adopted**

_____ copied   _____ celebrated

_____ accepted   _____ presented

3:2 Making Connections

The vocabulary words in the sentences below are taken from the reading passage. For each vocabulary word, choose a synonym and an antonym from the list that follows. Write the synonyms and antonyms in the blanks.

modest   distributed   easy   rejected   plentifulness

difficult   lack   assumed   kept   boastful

1. Work began on the uniforms in late January, but they were not **issued** until the summer.

synonym: _____   antonym: _____

2. The months during Jack's illness were **trying** ones for his family.

synonym: _____   antonym: _____

3. A **humble** woman, Mrs. Rodriguez did not talk about the patience and imagination she employed in her work with handicapped children.

synonym: _____ antonym: _____

4. The **abundance** of the country's food supply should ensure that everyone has enough to eat.

synonym: _____ antonym: _____

5. The Wongs **adopted** a family policy of leaving an extra house key with the next-door neighbor.

synonym: _____ antonym: _____

3:3 Making Connections
Write each vocabulary word on the line in front of the appropriate synonym and antonym.

issued	trying	humble	abundance	adopted

	synonym	antonym
1. _____	simple	grand
2. _____	accepted	rejected
3. _____	circulated	collected
4. _____	taxing	easy
5. _____	plenty	scarcity

3:4 Making Connections
Complete the following analogies by inserting one of the five vocabulary words in the blank at the end of each one. Remember that in an analogy the last two words or phrases must be related to each other in the same way that the first two are related. The colon in an analogy is read "is to," and the symbol :: is read "as." So "high:low::wide:narrow" would be read "high is to low as wide is to narrow."

issued	trying	humble	abundance	adopted

1. George Washington:honest::Abraham Lincoln: _____

2. full:overflowing::excess: _____

3. book:published::coin: _____

4. acquired:bought::taken on: _____

5. valuable:worthless::effortless: _____

4: The Roots of Our Language

re- The prefix *re-* is one of the most common in the English language. It comes from a Latin word meaning back or again. *Re-* appears in dozens of words you already know. *Repay,* for instance, means to pay back, and *redo* means to do again. If you wanted to check to make sure that you had counted a group of items correctly, you might recount them, which means, of course, that you would count them again. *Recount* has another meaning. It can mean to tell about something, such as an event, in detail. A person might recount the adventures he or she had on vacation.

ply *Reply* means to answer. A reply, then, is something said back. The word is made up of the prefix *re-* and the root *ply,* which means fold. *Reply* grew out of the Latin word *replicare,* which means to fold back. The Italians also took that Latin word into their language, and they gave it the meaning to repeat. From that word we got the English words *replica* and *replicate.* A replica is a copy or reproduction of something. It is something that is repeated, or made again. A statue, for example, that is made to look just like an original work of art is a replica. So is a piece of modern furniture that is made to look like a piece of furniture from two hundred years ago. To replicate is to make a replica—to make a copy.

cedere Remembering that *re-* means back, let's look at the word *recede.* To *recede* is to withdraw, or to move back or away. The tide recedes, or goes out. Roads appear to recede into the distance. *Recede* has a Latin root—*recedere,* meaning to go back. The *cedere* part, as you might guess, means to go. A related word that you are certainly familiar with is *recess.* When students have a recess, they take a break from their studies. When the United States Congress recesses, the senators and representatives stop meeting for a while. A recess is a time when work stops. It is a "going back" from work. *Recess* also has another meaning. A place in a wall that is set back from the rest of the wall is a recess.

pro- Another common word that has the same root as *recede* and *recess* is *proceed,* which means to go forward. The prefix *pro-* means forward. A *procedure* is a set of actions done in a particular order, or a way of accomplishing something. A procedure moves from a beginning to an end. A process, then, is something that is proceeding, or going on.

To move to a new root, let's look at another *re-* word: *recluse.* A recluse is a person who chooses to live alone, apart from society. Some recluses separate themselves from other people for religious reasons, as monks do. Others live by themselves just because they prefer to be alone. You might remember that *-clu* means shut, as in the verb *closet,* which means to shut away. A prisoner, who is *forced* to live outside society, is not a recluse.

-ject When someone rejects something, he refuses to accept it. Since the *-ject* means to throw or to force, *reject* means, literally, to throw back. The root *-ject* also appears in the word *inject.* To inject means to force into. When a doctor gives an injection, he or she uses a needle to force a liquid into the patient. Inject also has a nonmedical meaning. It can mean to introduce a new idea or element into something else. If you introduce a new idea into a conversation, for instance, you are injecting your thoughts.

Now as you do the exercises related to this lesson, try to recall what you have read.

4:1   Write each word or root listed on the left beside its meaning on the right.

re-

inject

ply

recede

pro-

1. _____ fold

2. _____ forward

3. _____ to go back

4. _____ to force into

5. _____ back or again

4:2   Mark each statement as either true or false.

_____   1. A prisoner alone in his cell is a recluse.

_____   2. A procedure is a set of actions done in a particular order.

_____   3. A rejected offer is one that is immediately accepted.

_____   4. A doctor or a nurse will use a needle to give an ejection.

_____   5. A replica is supposed to look just like another object.

4:3   Put an *x* in front of the answer choice you think is correct.

1. When Congress stops work for a week, they declare a

☐ a. recluse.   ☐ b. recount.   ☐ c. recess.

2. At low tide, the water at a beach

☐ a. recedes.   ☐ b. recesses.   ☐ c. replies.

3. If you enter a drawing contest and your entry is rejected, you

☐ a. win first prize.   ☐ b. do not get a prize.   ☐ c. can enter again.

4. If you're told to do a job a certain way, you are being asked to follow a

☐ a. procedure.   ☐ b. recession.   ☐ c. replica.

5. Someone who decides to live alone is a

☐ a. reject.   ☐ b. recluse.   ☐ c. procluse.

5:Extending Your Word Power

5:1 Multiple Meanings

Some of the vocabulary words you met in this unit have meanings other than those they held in the reading passages. Below, two or three definitions are shown for each of the words *fixed* and *trying*. Next to each sentence, write the letter of the definition that matches the way in which the vocabulary word is used in the sentence.

fixed

a. (adj.) not movable

b. (adj.) settled; set

c. (v.) repaired

_____ 1. The buoy is anchored in a **fixed** position in the harbor.

_____ 2. That is a **fixed** price; there is no room for bargaining.

_____ 3. After Sally had **fixed** the chain on her bicycle, she was covered with grease.

trying

a. (v.) attempting

b. (adj.) annoying; hard to bear

_____ 4. Because Gary's mother finds the sound of rock music **trying**, she asks Gary to wear headphones when listening to his stereo.

_____ 5. **Trying** too hard at something can lead to frustration.

_____ 6. After a **trying** day, Mr. Conrad likes to sit back and read a good book.

5:2 Roots Review

The incomplete sentences below contain words that you learned in the two roots lessons in this unit. Complete each sentence so that it makes sense and shows the meaning of the boldfaced vocabulary word.

1. To **decode** the message, which was written in numbers, Lou had to _____

_____ .

2. When Stephanie read her pay stub, she was amazed that the **deductions** _____

_____ .

3. From the fact that the jewels were missing but the lock on the case had not been broken, Detective

Shultz **deduced** _____

_____ .

4. In order to **detect** intruders in the castle, Lord Stanton _____ _____ .

5. We begged the old man to **recount** his experiences in Africa, so he finally _____ _____ .

6. The antique cupboard was difficult to **replicate** because _____ _____ .

7. Amy felt sad as she watched the boat **recede**, because _____ _____ .

8. Arthur's **deduction** that Harold was avoiding him was _____ _____ .

9. Martha was so eager to **inject** her opinion that _____ _____ .

10. Colin explained that following **procedure** was important because _____ _____ .

5:3 Choosing Just the Right Word

Remember that the best writers, the best communicators, take care to choose just the right words to express their ideas. They don't say *happy* if they mean *elated,* or *angry* if they mean *irritated.* You too should be as clear and precise as you can be when you speak and write.

Below are synonym studies for two of your vocabulary words. One compares and contrasts the meanings of *restore, renew* and *repair.* The other looks at the difference between *trying* and *difficult.* Read the studies closely to learn what the differences are between the synonyms. Then use the vocabulary words and their synonyms to complete the sentences that follow. In some cases you may need to use a past tense. Use the synonym studies to help you select the best word for each sentence.

restore   renew   repair

Restore, renew and *repair* all have to do with fixing things. *Restore* is used when speaking of working on old buildings and furniture to make them look exactly as they did when they were new. *The Westons restored the run-down farmhouse in the style of the 1850s, when it was built.* **Renew** means to make something fresh or complete again. *Janet's confidence was renewed when she got the part she wanted in the play.* To repair is to fix a damaged or broken item. *Jack had to repair the broken window.*

trying   difficult

Trying and *difficult* both mean hard to do or to deal with. *Difficult* means hard to do, to figure out, to understand, or to accomplish. It implies the need to do something: to overcome an obstacle, to learn something, or to solve a problem. With a difficulty, patience, skill or courage are usually required. *Hal finds algebra difficult, so he spends more time studying it than he does other subjects. Trying* means upsetting, or especially hard to bear or put up with. It also means annoying. Something that is trying calls for no action. It just has to be lived through, put up with, avoided, or done away with. *Cindy found her little brother's teasing so trying that she went to her room and closed the door. Helen finds the pressure of her work so trying that she is looking for a less demanding job.*

1. After it was _____ , the roll-top desk looked just as it had when Celia's grandfather made it.

2. Greg found it _____ to listen to Ellen's bad jokes and puns.

3. The brakes on Joshua's bicycle were sticking, so he had to _____ them.

4. All Mrs. Lopez needed to _____ her energy after her long trip was a hot bath and a good night's sleep.

5. Pat found it _____ to build a coop for her rabbits, but she stuck with the project until it was finished and her pets had a new home.

5:4 Recognizing Other Word Forms

The words below are other forms of the vocabulary words you have worked with in this unit. Fill in the blank in each sentence with the appropriate word. If you are unsure of the meaning of a word, refer to the glossary.

adoption   humility   fixedly   restoration   merely   abundant

1. The _____ of the old train station had hardly begun when a proposal was brought before the city council to build a new one instead.

2. Though the poet was internationally famous, her _____ came across in the simple, quiet way in which she spoke.

3. The Russian immigrants were shocked by the _____ supply of food available in every grocery store in the United States.

4. Michael sat _____ waiting for more than an hour for the results of his history exam.

5. Most of the seventh-graders voted against the _____ of a rule

outlawing balls on the school grounds.

6. Antonio thought of Maria as a close friend, not _____ as a cousin.

5:5 Putting Your Vocabulary to Use

In solving this word puzzle, you will be using some of the vocabulary words introduced in this unit and in the last unit. Below is a list of definitions and synonyms for those words. For each definition or synonym, think of a vocabulary word that has the same meaning. Write the word in the puzzle space with the same number. The circled letter, together with the number of lines in each answer space, provide clues to the word. Notice that the circled letters form a phrase related to Lincoln. Write the phrase on the line provided.

1. not grand; modest and unassuming
2. translate a secret message
3. difficult or wearing
4. belongings
5. make up for a debt
6. plentifulness
7. copy of an original
8. lived in
9. incorrect; not proper
10. come to an end
11. withdraw or move back
12. work or study break
13. stationary
14. take away
15. put into circulation
16. a conclusion reached through reasoning
17. brief period in between

1. _ _ _ _ ⓛ _

2. _ _ _ _ ⓞ _ _ _

3. _ _ _ _ _ _ ⓖ

4. _ _ _ _ ⓒ _ _

5. _ _ _ _ ⓐ _

6. _ ⓑ _ _ _ _ _ _ _

7. _ _ _ _ ⓘ _ _

8. _ ⓝ _ _ _ _ _ _

9. _ _ ⓟ _ _ _ _

10. _ _ _ _ ⓡ _

11. _ _ _ _ _ ⓔ

12. _ _ _ _ ⓢ _

13. _ ⓘ _ _ _

14. _ _ ⓓ _ _ _

15. _ _ _ _ ⓔ

16. _ _ _ _ _ _ _ _ ⓝ

17. _ _ ⓣ _ _ _ _ _ _

Phrase: _____

UNIT 5

1: Meeting Words in Context

Reading Selection   Babe Didrikson

Words Introduced   innate adept diligence prevailing
succumb

2: The Roots of Our Language

Roots Introduced   trans- -port ex- im- re- -fer
pre- con-

3: Meeting Words in Context

Reading Selection   The Birth of Basketball

Words Introduced   vigorous incorporate propel affixed
delineating

4: The Roots of Our Language

Roots Introduced   inter- -sect bi- fere

5: Extending Your Word Power

Multiple Meanings
Roots Review
Using Words Precisely
Recognizing Other Word Forms
Putting Your Vocabulary to Use

1:Meeting Words in Context

Babe Didrikson

At age eighteen, Mildred Didrikson took the sports world by surprise. She entered the 1932 Olympic Games in Los Angeles a virtual unknown and finished with two gold medals. She would have had a third, in the high jump, but she was disqualified for making an unusual jump. The method she used was later legalized. That same year, in the Amateur Athletic Union championships, she won five events and tied for first place in the high jump. In 1950, Babe Didrikson, as she was known, was named the outstanding woman athlete of the first half of the twentieth century by the Associated Press.

Born in Texas of Norwegian immigrant parents, Babe was encouraged in outdoor exercise throughout her childhood. In addition to her **innate** athletic abilities, she had a powerful urge to do things better than anyone else. **Adept** at tennis, basketball, track and field, golf, swimming, and baseball, Babe decided to concentrate her energies on one sport. She chose golf.

Babe's driving power in golf was unbeatable from the start. She applied herself to learning the game thoroughly, and her **diligence** produced results. She was soon winning amateur tournaments right and left. In 1946 she won the U.S. Women's Amateur tournament. Then in 1947 she went on to win a record seventeen consecutive major women's golf tournaments, including the British Ladies' Amateur. She was the first American to take that prize.

To her outstanding record as an amateur athlete, Babe then added a substantial number of professional victories. She won the U.S. Women's Open three times, **prevailing** over some excellent golfers.

In the early fifties, Babe's life and career were disrupted by illness—first a hernia, then a more serious condition, eventually diagnosed as cancer. In 1954, after surgery, she returned to the golf circuit. It was then that she won her third U.S. Open. But her return to sports was brief. The cancer resurfaced. At forty-five, Babe Didrikson, the superwoman of sports, **succumbed** to the disease. She died on September 27, 1956. Some say she was as great an athlete as the world has ever known.

Choose from the story two words that are unfamiliar to you or whose meanings you are not completely sure of. (Do not choose words that appear in boldfaced type.) Write the words on the lines provided below. Then, beside each word, write what you think it means, based on how it was used in the story.

1. _____ : _____

   _____

2. _____ : _____

   _____

When you have finished the exercises in this lesson, go to your dictionary and find the definitions for the words you entered above. If a word has more than one meaning, look for the one that defines the word as it is used in the story. Then write the words and their dictionary definitions in the Student Words pages at the back of the book. How close did you come to figuring out their meanings for yourself?

1:1 Using Context

Put an *x* in the box beside each correct answer. For clues to the meanings of the words, reread the parts of the passage in which they appear.

1. **Innate** abilities are abilities that
   ☐ a. no one is aware of.
   ☐ b. prove intelligence.
   ☐ c. one is born with.
   ☐ d. are learned over time.

2. To be **adept** at many sports means to
   ☐ a. be unable to choose among them.
   ☐ b. be familiar with but not good at them.
   ☐ c. dislike them.
   ☐ d. be skilled at them.

3. Since in the sentence with the word *diligence* we are told that Babe applied herself thoroughly to learning the game of golf, **diligence** must be
   ☐ a. technique.
   ☐ b. hard work and perseverance.
   ☐ c. intelligence.
   ☐ d. fun and lightheartedness.

4. Since we are told that Babe won by "prevailing over excellent golfers," we can infer that **prevailing** has to do with
   ☐ a. offering congratulations.
   ☐ b. playing fair.
   ☐ c. giving up.
   ☐ d. coming out ahead.

5. To **succumb** to a disease means to
   ☐ a. die from it.
   ☐ b. fight against it.
   ☐ c. learn about it.
   ☐ d. recover from it.

1:2 Making Connections

For each boldfaced word in the sentences below, choose a synonym and an antonym from the list that follows. Write the synonyms and antonyms in the blanks.

effort	skilled	yielded	inept	acquired
inborn	conquered	laziness	losing	succeeding

1. In addition to her **innate** athletic abilities, she had a powerful urge to do things better than anyone else.

   synonym: _____   antonym: _____

2. **Adept** at tennis, basketball, track and field, golf, swimming, and baseball, Babe decided to concentrate her energies on one sport.

   synonym: _____   antonym: _____

3. She applied herself to learning the game thoroughly, and her **diligence** produced results.

   synonym: _____   antonym: _____

4. She won the U. S. Women's Open three times, **prevailing** over some excellent golfers.

   synonym: _____ **antonym:** _____

5. At forty-five, Babe Didrickson, the superwoman of sports, **succumbed** to the disease.

   synonym: _____ **antonym:** _____

1:3 Making Connections
Complete the following analogies by inserting one of the five vocabulary words in the blank at the end of each one. Remember that in an analogy the last two words or phrases must be related in the same way that the first two are related.

innate   adept   diligence   prevail   succumb

1. ugliness : beauty : : laziness : _____

2. create : destroy : : overcome : _____

3. subject : knowledgeable : : skill : _____

4. job : succeed : : contest : _____

5. awkward : graceful : : acquired : _____

1:4 Making Connections
Complete each sentence with the correct vocabulary word.

innate   adept   diligence   prevailing   succumbed

1. Samantha was _____ at passing notes in class without getting caught.

2. West High took the soccer championship for 1986, _____ over the two teams that had tied for first place the previous year.

3. Because of his _____ sense of direction, Henry was always elected to lead the way on hiking expeditions.

4. After twitching on the dock for almost an hour, the fish finally _____ .

5. It was only with the greatest _____ that Vanessa was able to overcome her stuttering.

2: The Roots of Our Language

trans-
-port

You probably know that *transport* means to carry something from one place to another. The prefix *trans-* means across or beyond, and the root *-port* means to carry. A porter is a person who carries things for other people. Porters at airports, for instance, have the job of carrying people's baggage.

The root *-port* also means harbor or gate. The place in which ships anchor may be called either a harbor or a port. The places where airplanes land and are kept is, of course, called an airport. Likewise, space vehicles are kept in spaceports.

ex-
im-

It is from ports of various kinds that goods are exported and imported—sent out and taken in. The prefix *ex-* means out of or from, and the prefix *im-* means in. So an export is something that is sent out, and an import is something that is brought in.

re-

At various points during a school year, students receive report cards. A report is information sent back to someone. *Re-* means back or again. Travelers report on the places they've seen and the things they've done on their travels. Journalists report events.

-fer

Transfer has a meaning that is similar to the meaning of *transport*. Like *-port*, *-fer* means carry, or bear. Both *transport* and *transfer* refer to moving things, but *transport* refers to the action of actually carrying something somewhere, while *transfer* refers to the changing of location without mention of the actual carrying. A company might transfer a worker from the east coast to the west coast, for example, but the worker has to be transported to the new place. In traveling long distances by air, passengers sometimes have to transfer from one airplane to another. They would be transported from one plane to another only if they were given a ride in some sort of vehicle. If you sell a car to someone, you transfer the title, or ownership papers, to the new owner, which means you turn the papers over to the person. This can be done in person or through the mail. As you can see from these examples, a transfer is a kind of exchange: one place to another, one vehicle to another, one person to another.

pre-

Another word that contains the root *-fer* is *prefer*, meaning to like better, or to choose over something else. For instance, some people prefer chocolate cake to apple pie. *Pre-*, as you'll recall, means before. So *prefer* literally means to put one thing before another.

Infer is another word with the same root. The root *-fer* plus the prefix *in-* means to carry or bring into. The dictionary definition of *infer* is "to figure out by reasoning; to conclude." When we see smoke, for instance, we infer fire. To the facts that we are given (the sight of smoke, in this example), we bring or carry some of our own knowledge—in this case, the knowledge that smoke is produced by fire. You make inferences all the time. If you see tire tracks in the snow, you infer that a vehicle has passed by. If you're playing your radio loudly and a man says, "Gee, that music sure is loud," you can infer that he'd like you to lower the volume.

con-

Finally, let's look at *confer*. As you learned in Unit 1, *con-* means together. When *con-* is joined to *-fer*, we get the meaning "to bring together." To confer is to compare ideas. In other words, to bring ideas together. A conference is a meeting at which two or more people discuss matters that concern them all.

2:1   Write each word or root listed on the left beside its meaning on the right.

trans-   1. _____   to carry or to bear

port   2. _____   out of or from

ex-   3. _____   in

im-   4. _____   harbor

-fer   5. _____   across or beyond

2:2   Mark each statement as either true or false.

_____   1. A landing and taking off place for a helicopter is called a heliport.

_____   2. A policewoman who is sent from one precinct to another across town has been given a transfer.

_____   3. An import is something that cannot be brought in from another place.

_____   4. When a person sells a house, he turns over the deed to the new owner. In other words, the two people transport the deed.

_____   5. When the United States takes in coffee beans from South America, the United States imports those beans.

2:3   Put an *x* in front of the answer choice you think is correct.

1. A radio message that is sent across the ocean from England to America could be called

   ☐ a. transatlantic.   ☐ b. transported.   ☐ c. exported.

2. A building that explodes sends particles hurtling out, so a building that collapses in on itself, sending particles inward is said to

   ☐ a. deplode.   ☐ b. implode.   ☐ c. unplode.

3. Since *-port* means to carry and *-able* means capable of, it stands to reason that *portable* means capable of

   ☐ a. standing still.   ☐ b. being carried.   ☐ c. generating power.

4. Newspaper people who observe events, write about those events, and send what they've written back to their papers are called

   ☐ a. readers.   ☐ b. printers.   ☐ c. reporters.

5. You know that *hale* comes from a root that means to breathe, and you know that *ex-* means out of. To breathe out, then, is to

   ☐ a. inhale.   ☐ b. expire.   ☐ c. exhale.

3: Meeting Words in Context

The Birth of Basketball

Unlike most sports, which evolved over time from street games, basketball was designed by one man to suit a particular purpose. The man was Dr. James Naismith, and his purpose was to invent a **vigorous** game that could be played indoors during the winter.

In 1891, Naismith was an instructor at the International YMCA Training School, now Springfield College, in Massachusetts. The school trained physical education instructors for YMCAs throughout the country. That year the school was trying to come up with a physical activity that the men could enjoy between the football and baseball seasons. None of the standard indoor activities held their interest for long. Naismith was asked to solve the problem.

He first tried to adapt some of the popular outdoor sports, but they were all too rough. The men were getting bruised from tackling each other and being hit with equipment. Windows were getting smashed.

Finally Naismith decided to try to invent a game that would **incorporate** the most common elements of outdoor team sports without the physical contact. He noted that most of the popular sports used a ball. He chose a soccer ball, because it was soft and large enough that it required no equipment, such as a bat or a racket, to **propel** it. That ensured that the ball wouldn't travel too fast. Next he decided on an elevated goal, so that scoring would depend on skill and accuracy rather than on brute strength. His goals were two peach baskets, **affixed** to ten-foot-high balconies at each end of the gym. Naismith then wrote thirteen rules **delineating** the specifics of the game. Many of those rules are still in effect.

Basketball was an immediate success. The students taught it to their friends, and the new sport quickly caught on. Folks have been dribbling ever since.

Choose from the story two words that are unfamiliar to you or whose meanings you are not completely sure of. (Do not choose words that appear in boldfaced type.) Write the words on the lines provided below. Then, beside each word, write what you think it means, based on how it was used in the story.

1. _____ : _____

   _____

2. _____ : _____

   _____

When you have finished the exercises in this lesson, go to your dictionary and find the definitions for the words you entered above. If a word has more than one meaning, look for the one that defines the word as it is used in the story. Then write the words and their dictionary definitions in the Student Words pages at the back of the book. How close did you come to figuring out their meanings for yourself?

3:1 Using Context

Below are five sentences from the reading passage. From the four choices that follow each sentence, choose the one that gives the best definition of the boldfaced word. Put an *x* in the box beside it. Use the context, or setting, provided by the sentence to help you discover the meaning of the word. If the sentence itself does not provide enough clues, go back to the passage and read the paragraph in which the sentence appears.

1. The man was Dr. James Naismith, and his purpose was to invent a **vigorous** game that could be played indoors during the winter.
   - ☐ a. physically active and energetic
   - ☐ b. complex
   - ☐ c. violent
   - ☐ d. slow and easygoing

2. Finally Naismith decided to try to invent a game that would **incorporate** the most common elements of outdoor team sports without the physical contact.
   - ☐ a. leave out of the game
   - ☐ b. define
   - ☐ c. change around
   - ☐ d. work into the game

3. He chose a soccer ball, because it was soft and large enough that it required no equipment, such as a bat or a racket, to **propel** it.
   - ☐ a. hit it properly
   - ☐ b. break it apart
   - ☐ c. drive it forward
   - ☐ d. hold it tightly

4. His goals were two peach baskets, **affixed** to ten-foot-high balconies at each end of the gym.
   - ☐ a. fastened securely
   - ☐ b. painted onto
   - ☐ c. built into
   - ☐ d. draped loosely over

5. Naismith then wrote thirteen rules **delineating** the specifics of the game.
   - ☐ a. lining up side by side
   - ☐ b. describing in detail
   - ☐ c. examining
   - ☐ d. researching

3:2 Making Connections

Write each vocabulary word on the line in front of the appropriate synonym and antonym.

vigorous   incorporate   propel   affix   delineate

	synonym	antonym
1. _____	attach	remove
2. _____	energetic	slow-moving
3. _____	include	eliminate
4. _____	push	pull
5. _____	specify	generalize

3:3 Making Connections

Complete the following analogies by inserting one of the five vocabulary words in the blank at the end of each one. Remember that in an analogy the last two words or phrases must be related in the same way that the first two are related.

vigorous   incorporating   propel   affixed   delineate

1. clasp : hold : : push : _____

2. questions : inquire : : definitions : _____

3. boring : dull : : energetic : _____

4. increasing : enlarging : : including : _____

5. dug : filled in : : removed : _____

3:4 Making Connections

Complete each sentence with the correct vocabulary word.

vigorous   incorporate   propel   affixed   delineating

1. Jeannie crouched at the starting line, ready to _____ herself forward the moment she heard the gun.

2. As supervisor of the group, Hank was assigned the task of _____ the procedure that was to be followed in carrying out the operation.

3. Mr. Wilcox decided to _____ a touch of elegance into his homey, unpretentious restaurant.

4. _____ to the bumper of the car in front of Mariel was a sticker that read, "If you can read this, you're too close."

5. The stain that Violet was using on her bookcase would not come off her hands without a _____ scrubbing.

4: The Roots of Our Language

inter-
The prefix *inter-,* meaning between, forms the beginning of many common words. *International,* for instance, means between nations, and *interaction* means action between people. A science fiction character who engages in interstellar travel travels between or among the stars. *Stella* is Latin for star.

An intersection of two roads is the place where two roads cross. To intersect means to divide by passing through or across. If you draw two circles and one passes through part of the other, the circles are said to intersect. The area that they share is called an intersection. The root *-sect* means to cut. At an intersection, one thing cuts through another.

-sect

bi-
To bisect means to cut in two. The prefix *bi-* means two, as in bicycle, which is a two-wheeled vehicle. If you cut an orange in half, you bisect it.

If you ask someone a lot of questions, you are interrogating him. *Interrogate* means to question thoroughly to obtain information. Spy movies and detective shows often have a character who acts as an interrogator—a person who questions, or interrogates, a suspected criminal. The root *roga* comes from the Latin word *rogare,* meaning to ask. An interrogative (int-uh-ROG-uh-tiv) sentence is one that asks a question. Such a sentence ends in an interrogation point, more commonly known as a question mark.

An interval is a space between two objects or a space in time between two events—a pause. If someone pauses before answering a question, there is an interval between the question and the answer. There is a six-day interval between Christmas and New Year's Day. Here is a sample sentence: *In the interval between periods of the hockey game, Jeff went to buy some popcorn.*

fere
While we're thinking about sports, let's look at the word *interfere,* which means to block or get in the way of, or to collide. In many sports, interference is the illegal blocking of another player. The root *fere* means to strike. So the first meaning of *interfere* was to strike one another. Of course, *interfere* is not just a sports word. It also has the general meaning of getting in the way of anything being accomplished, and of involving yourself in something that has nothing to do with you. For instance, if you try to get into the middle of someone else's argument, you might be told that you are interfering. Likewise, if someone turns on the television while you are doing homework, you might say, "You're interfering with my studying."

Football players often try to intercept a pass without committing interference. The general meaning of *intercept* is to take or grab something that is on its way from one place to another. Intercepting a pass, as you know if you are a football fan, is catching a ball that is being thrown between players on the other team.

Sports and exercise in general help to invigorate people. *Invigorate* means to give life and energy. If you're feeling tired, for instance, a hard, fast game of tennis or basketball will make you feel invigorated. *Vigor* itself means strength or force. It is also used to mean mental force and energy. A vigorous mind is one that is quick and active.

4:1 Write each word or root listed on the left beside its meaning on the right.

inter-

-sect

interval

interfere

invigorate

1. _____ to give life and energy

2. _____ a space in time between two events

3. _____ to block or get in the way of

4. _____ between

5. _____ to cut

4:2 Mark each statement as either true or false.

_____ 1. You could describe your summer vacation as the interval between two school years.

_____ 2. If you interfere with your friend's trumpet practice, you are blocking his progress on the instrument.

_____ 3. To be invigorated means to be tired, or out of vigor.

_____ 4. Parallel lines, which never meet, sometimes form intersections.

_____ 5. If you go for a vigorous walk, you take a lazy, carefree stroll.

4:3 Answer the following questions.

1. If you know that -*sect* means to cut, and that *dis*- means apart, what are you doing when you dissect a frog in biology class? _____

_____

2. Knowing that *inter*- means between, and that *view* comes from a word meaning to meet and talk, why do you think interviews, such as those you see on television, are called interviews? _____

_____

3. If you go to a double feature at a theater, what word from the lesson might you use to describe the period of time between the two movies? _____

_____

4. When your radio reception is broken up by static and other unwanted noise, why is that noise called interference? _____

_____

5. If your report card (which is not going to be so good this time) is mailed to your home, and you plan to take it from the mailbox before anyone can see it, you might say that you plan to _____ it.

5: Extending Your Word Power

5:1 Multiple Meanings

Some of the vocabulary words you met in this unit have more than one meaning. Three words and their definitions are listed below. In the sentences that follow, fill in the blanks with the correct vocabulary words. To determine which word belongs in each sentence, refer to the definitions that are given.

prevail

a. (v.) to gain a victory through strength

b. (v.) to use persuasion effectively

c. (v.) to be in use or fashion

incorporate

a. (v.) to work something in

b. (v.) to form into a legal corporation

delineate

a. (v.) to describe or set forth in detail

b. (v.) to indicate or mark the outline of

1. The police asked the Block Association to _____ their plans for a neighborhood crime-watch network.

2. Woody intended to _____ upon his mother until she gave him permission to join his friends on an overnight bike trip.

3. Mrs. Rodriguez planted a row of small rose bushes to _____ the property line between the two houses.

4. Paula and her partner, Diane, had no idea of the amount of work it would take to _____ their small crafts business.

5. Some of the formal social customs of an earlier era still _____ today among the wealthy old families of Europe.

6. Nina tried hard to _____ her ballet teacher's suggestions into her stage performance.

7. The excited spectators did not know which team would _____ until the final moment of the football game.

8. Theodore used a red felt-tip marker to _____ the pre-Civil War borders on his map.

9. Brown and Manor filed all the papers necessary to _____ their new law firm.

10. The president asked each state to _____ upon its citizens for their cooperation in minimizing the risks of accidents over the holiday weekend.

5:2 Roots Review
The incomplete sentences below contain words that you learned in the two roots lessons in this unit. Complete each sentence so that it makes sense and shows the meaning of the boldfaced vocabulary word.

1. To **transport** the heavy cannon, the soldiers _____

_____ .

2. Because Janice **preferred** baseball, _____

_____ .

3. Hiram's scheduled **conference** with the principal _____

_____ .

4. Before she could **transfer** the contents of her locker, _____

_____ .

5. This year's **International** Film Festival showed films from _____

_____ .

6. After a short **interval**, _____

_____ .

7. Rachel frowned and said, "Studying **interferes** _____

_____ ."

8. After **bisecting** the grapefruit, Sammy had _____

_____ .

9. **"Invigorating!"** Mr. Krunwaddle shouted. "That's what _____

_____ ."

10. The **interrogator** pulled at his mustache and _____

_____ .

5:3 Choosing Just the Right Word

Some of the words you have worked with in this unit have synonyms. The synonyms are slightly different in meaning from the vocabulary words. When you write and speak, it is up to you to choose the words that mean exactly what you want to say.

Below are synonym studies for three of the vocabulary words. Use either the vocabulary words or their synonyms to complete the sentences in the exercise that follows. Refer to the synonym studies as you decide which word carries the best meaning for the specific context of each sentence.

vigorous   strenuous

Vigorous and *strenuous* mean having or requiring great vitality or force. *Vigorous* implies showing no signs of lessening freshness or energy. *A vigorous walk stimulates blood circulation. Strenuous* suggests a difficult or challenging task that tests strength. *An excess of strenuous activity should be avoided by heart patients.*

1. Four hours of lifting proved too _____ for Anthony's weak back; he

spent the next day and a half in bed with a heating pad.

2. For the final selection, the conductor chose a _____ piece of music

that would leave the audience in high spirits.

3. The hikers trained long and hard for their _____ trek up the

mountain.

affix   attach

>*Affix* and *attach* mean to make something stay firmly connected to something else. *Affix* implies directly fixing one object to another, usually permanently, by such means as gluing, stamping or nailing. *Sidney affixed leather patches to the elbows of her jacket. Attach* suggests joining with the use of a link, tie, bolt, hinge or other connecting device. *The Joneses attached their camper to their car and set off for a two-week vacation.*

4. Gail used a shoestring to _____ her tricycle to her brother's wagon.

5. Applicants were asked to _____ a small black-and-white photo of themselves to their application forms using paper clips.

6. After ten hours of driving, Renee did not have the energy even to

_____ a stamp to an envelope.

propel   push

>*Propel* and *push* both mean to force to move forward or aside. *Propel* suggests driving something quickly forward or onward by any kind of strong force. *The gun propelled the bullet through the air. John propelled the puck across the ice with a swift slice of his hockey stick. Push* implies that the thing providing the force stays in steady contact with the object being moved. In other words, to push is to move by pressing. *Larry braced his hands against the piano and pushed the instrument across the room.*

7. When his car stalled and wouldn't start again, Dave had to get help to

_____ the car to the side of the road.

8. With his strong arm, Bruce could _____ a baseball faster than anyone else in the league.

9. To _____ the soccer ball across the field, Lucy gave it a powerful kick.

5:4 Recognizing Other Word Forms

Each sentence below requires you to use a different form of one of the words you have studied in this unit. The words you will need to fill in the blanks are listed below. If you are unsure of the meaning of a word, look it up in the glossary.

diligently   vigor   propulsion   innately   prevailed

incorporation   affixing   delineation   propeller   invigorating

1. Meredith knew that history was not an _____ boring subject, and she blamed her teacher for the class's lack of enthusiasm.

2. The Roths planned a little family ceremony for _____ the street numbers to their freshly-painted house.

3. The sailors returned to their ship with renewed _____ after three days of shore liberty.

4. In the end justice _____ , and the factory was shut down for management's refusal to comply with pollution-control regulations.

5. Bernard practiced his oboe _____ for several months, and by September he had improved enough to be accepted into the band.

6. Sean wound the _____ of his model airplane, let it go, and watched the plane crash immediately into the garage.

7. The new design for the train station reflected the _____ of the ideas of three architects into one plan.

8. Before she took the job as administrative assistant, Janet asked for a _____ of the responsibilities of the job.

9. Gladys and Herbert fantasized about an _____ canoe trip down white-water rapids, but they went to Miami instead.

10. The space launch was delayed because of a minor flaw in the jet _____ system.

5:5 Putting Your Vocabulary to Use

The scrambled words below are all vocabulary words from this unit or the last one. Use the definition or synonym next to each scramble to help you figure out what the word is. Then write the word in the space provided. The number of lines in each answer space also provides a clue to the word. The circled letters will form a phrase related to golf. Write that phrase on the line provided at the bottom of the puzzle.

1. TENANI   inborn   — — — — — —

2. ITHYMIUL   modesty   Ⓞ — — — — — — —

3. MCUSBUC   give in   — — — — — — —

4. PRNOARSTT   carry   — — — — — — Ⓞ — —

5. TERCJE   throw back   — — — — — —

6. VERPLAI   win   — — — — — Ⓞ

7. FERPER   like better   — — — — — —

8. REEM   only; simple   — Ⓞ — —

9. GROVI   energy   — Ⓞ — — —

10. RNIFE   to conclude from facts   — — — — —

11. USEUTSNOR   requiring great energy   — — — Ⓞ — — — —

12. XAFIF   attach   — — — — — —

13. OLERPP   drive forward   — — Ⓞ — — —

14. FNASRTER   pass on   — — — Ⓞ — — — —

15. TEEDCT   discover   — — — — — —

16. SEDROTER   renewed   — — — — — Ⓞ —

Phrase: _____

1: Meeting Words in Context

Reading Selection   The Robots Are Coming!

Words Introduced   credit   versatile   agile   intervals   offset

2: The Roots of Our Language

Roots Introduced   sub-   marine   merge   -tract   de-   re- scribe   mit

3: Meeting Words in Context

Reading Selection   The Future of Robotics

Words Introduced   executing   ultimately   relatively   inclined versed

4: The Roots of Our Language

Roots Introduced   over-   whelm

5: Extending Your Word Power

Multiple Meanings
Roots Review
Using Words Precisely
Recognizing Other Word Forms
Putting Your Vocabulary to Use

1: Meeting Words in Context

The Robots are Coming!

What can a robot do? Sorry to disappoint you, but if you thought that C3PO of *Star Wars* fame was what the robot of the future would be like, you're in for a few surprises.

The truth is that most robots do not even closely resemble humans. People often **credit** them with being far more intelligent than they actually are.

The brain of an individual robot is a computerized control box, or center, on top of which is one long arm. Why not two arms? Robot technology has not progressed beyond one arm.

That one arm is **versatile**—capable of moving up, down and around. Some highly **agile** robots have arms that can rotate in a full circle.

At the end of a robot's hand is a swivel wrist attached to a handlike device consisting of two claws or grips. Put a programmed robot on an assembly line, and its arm will work tirelessly at simple tasks traditionally performed by humans.

Robots can be programmed to use heavy welding guns and spray paint, to remove castings from hot furnaces, and to install precision parts.

The more intelligent ones can actually perform several chores, such as selecting tools from a rack and punching holes in a metal sheet.

Aside from having just one arm, robots have other limitations. They can neither see nor feel, so they won't get out of your way; you have to be careful to stay out of theirs. Once a robot is programmed on an assembly line, nothing will stop it, short of pulling the plug. Robots also cannot correct their mistakes. If faulty parts happen to be fed to them, they'll install them. So if a robot is busily welding on an auto assembly line, parts have to be timed to arrive at exact **intervals**. Otherwise, the robot will weld whatever is in front of it.

Yet the advantages of using robots more than **offset** their shortcomings. You won't find a robot complaining about the boredom of working on an assembly line, unpleasant working conditions, or too few breaks.

Reprinted from *Real World*, with special permission of King Features Syndicate, Inc.

Choose from the story two words that are unfamiliar to you or whose meanings you are not completely sure of. (Do not choose words that appear in boldfaced type.) Write the words on the lines provided below. Then, beside each word, write what you think it means, based on how it was used in the story.

1. _____ : _____

   _____

2. _____ : _____

   _____

When you have finished the exercises in this lesson, go to your dictionary and find the definitions for the words you entered above. If a word has more than one meaning, look for the one that defines the word as it is used in the story. Then write the words and their dictionary definitions in the Student Words pages at the back of the book. How close did you come to figuring out their meanings for yourself?

1:1 Using Context

Put an *x* in the box beside each correct answer. For clues to the meanings of the words, reread the parts of the passage in which they appear.

1. To **credit** robots with being more intelligent than they really are is to
   - ☐ a. pay more money for smarter robots.
   - ☐ b. doubt the intelligence of robots.
   - ☐ c. believe they are more intelligent.
   - ☐ d. build robots with more intelligence.

2. An arm that is **versatile** is
   - ☐ a. able to move in many different directions.
   - ☐ b. stronger than average.
   - ☐ c. weaker than average.
   - ☐ d. limited in its movements.

3. A highly **agile** robot is one that
   - ☐ a. is very clumsy.
   - ☐ b. has more than one arm.
   - ☐ c. moves in circles continuously.
   - ☐ d. moves with great ease.

4. Exact **intervals** are
   - ☐ a. set periods of time.
   - ☐ b. parts of an assembly line.
   - ☐ c. robots called intervals.
   - ☐ d. areas of the factory.

5. To say that the advantages **offset** the shortcomings of using robots means that the advantages
   - ☐ a. point out the shortcomings.
   - ☐ b. make up for the shortcomings.
   - ☐ c. delay the shortcomings.
   - ☐ d. are hidden by the shortcomings.

1:2 Making Connections

Listed below are the five vocabulary words from the reading passage, followed by ten words or phrases that are related to them in some way. The ten words and phrases may be synonyms, antonyms or definitions. On the line next to each word or phrase, write the vocabulary word that is related to it.

credit   versatile   agile   interval   offset

1. clumsy _____

2. attribute to _____

3. space _____

4. fall short of _____

5. compensate for _____

6. time period _____

7. multitalented _____

8. surefooted _____

9. deny _____

10. limited _____

1:3 Making Connections

Complete the following analogies by inserting one of the five vocabulary words in the blank at the end of each one. Remember that in an analogy the last two words or phrases must be related in the same way that the first two are related.

credit   versatile   agile   interval   offset

1. dancer : graceful : : acrobat : _____

2. dull : bright : : limited : _____

3. edge : brink : : space : _____

4. reveal : disclose : : counterbalance : _____

5. demand : request : : blame : _____

1:4 Making Connections

Complete each sentence with the correct vocabulary word.

credit   agile   versatile   interval   offset

1. Margaret, the most _____ of the three musicians, could play the violin, the cello and the piano.

2. The Krauses' new house was a forty-five minute ride from the city, but the inconvenience of the distance was _____ by the charm of the house and its surroundings.

3. The _____ children leapt easily from rock to rock along the shore.

4. An _____ of three years passed before the sisters saw each other again.

5. At the school assembly, Mr. Anton took time to _____ each student club for its hard work and creative efforts.

2: The Roots of Our Language

sub-
marine

A submarine travels under the water, and that is just what the parts of its name mean. The prefix *sub-* means under, and the root *marine* means sea.

As an adjective, the English word *marine* means of the sea. Marine life, for instance, is another way of saying life of the sea. It is a term used to refer to the creatures that live in the sea. A marine life aquarium is an aquarium for sea creatures. A related word is *marina* (muh-REE-nuh). A marina is a dock or harbor where boats can tie up and where supplies are available for small boats. A mariner (MAR-uh-ner) is a seaman or a sailor.

merge

When submarines go below the water, we say that they submerge. The root *merge* means to plunge or dive. So *submerge* naturally means to dive under. If you go underwater when you are swimming, you submerge yourself. When you wash dishes, you submerge them in the water in the dishpan.

Today we use the word *merge* to mean to combine, or to cause to be swallowed up or absorbed. It is often used when referring to the buying of one company by another, often larger, one. How did that meaning come from a root meaning dive? Well, one of the earliest meanings of *merge,* when it came into the English language, was drown. (It's easy to see how that meaning came from dive or plunge.) As the word later developed new meanings, it came to be used to describe the legal action whereby a small business was taken over, or absorbed, by a larger one. The small business was drowned, in a sense, by the large one. It lost its own identity. The smaller company sank and disappeared. Such a combining is called a merger.

-tract

To subtract, as you know, means to take away. The root *-tract* means draw. The Latin word *subtractus,* from which we got *subtract,* means to draw from beneath, or to withdraw. Another word that is based on the root *-tract* is

de-

detract. The prefix *de-,* as you may remember, means away. To detract means to draw, or take, away a part of something. It is often used to mean taking away quality or value from something. Flaking paint, for instance, detracts from the appearance of a house. Likewise, thorns do not detract from the beauty of a rose.

re-

Since the prefix *re-* means back, you might guess that the word *retract* means to draw, or take, back. If you say something that you didn't mean to say, you might wish that you could retract your words. Newspapers sometimes print retractions when they have published something that is untrue. In that kind of retraction, the newspaper apologizes and corrects the error that it made.

scribe

If you subscribe to a newspaper, you have it delivered to you. To subscribe is to promise to accept and pay for. The root *scribe* means write. A subscriber takes out a subscription by signing an agreement. This meaning of *subscribe* comes from the original meaning of the word, which was to sign one's name to a document or letter to show agreement or approval. It was from that meaning that we got still another meaning, which is to approve or agree. If you subscribe to someone's opinion on a subject, you agree with him or her.

mit

To subscribe to a magazine or newspaper, you have to submit a signed subscription form. To submit is to deliver formally—to give over. *Mit* is from the Latin word *mittere,* meaning to send. Another word with the same root is *remit.* Since one of the meanings of *re-* is back, *remit* means to send back. Subscribers must remit payment for the material for which they have subscribed.

2:1 Write each word or root listed on the left beside its meaning on the right.

sub-   1. _____ show agreement or approval

marine   2. _____ under

submerge   3. _____ to dive under

scribe   4. _____ of the sea

subscribe   5. _____ write

2:2 Mark each statement as either true or false.

_____ 1. The vessels known as submarines can travel on the surface of the water only.

_____ 2. If you agree with someone on an issue, you submerge to their point of view.

_____ 3. *Scribe* is another word for dive.

_____ 4. A mariner is a person who specializes in navigating over land.

_____ 5. To subscribe to a magazine is to sign up to have the magazine delivered to your home.

2:3 Put an *x* in front of the answer choice you think is correct.

1. A person who works as a crew member on a submarine is known as a

   ☐ a. private.   ☐ b. submariner.   ☐ c. subscriber.

2. Before the invention of the printing press, people were employed as writers to copy material by hand; they were known as

   ☐ a. scribes.   ☐ b. marines.   ☐ c. mergers.

3. A being that is less than human is known as a

   ☐ a. superhuman.   ☐ b. extrahuman.   ☐ c. subhuman.

4. One who signs a form agreeing to have a newspaper delivered is a

   ☐ a. subscriber.   ☐ b. scribe.   ☐ c. submerger.

5. If you are swimming without any kind of scuba gear, and you submerge, you had better

   ☐ a. float on   ☐ b. swim fast.   ☐ c. hold your breath.
   your back.

3: Meeting Words in Context

The Future of Robotics

Though industrial robots are still in a primitive stage, scientists have high aspirations for future generations of robots. Two arms, capable of **executing** separate tasks at the same time, is one goal. Beyond that, there is no telling just how complex these computer-operated helpers could **ultimately** become.

A new breed of technician-engineers called robotics specialists are already designing a new kind of robot. Though robotics is a **relatively** new field, the demand for robotics experts will increase as more industries begin to see the potential applications for robots in their manufacturing operations. Over the next few years we can expect a 35- to 40-percent growth in the robot industry, according to Angel Jordan, dean of engineering at Carnegie-Mellon University.

Right now, robots are a $185-million industry, with over 6,200 of them working in plants in the United States. Robotics experts predict that by the year 2000 robots will make up 5 percent of the American work force.

The world leader in robot technology is Japan, with 21,000 robots working in its factories. While robot technology is becoming more sophisticated and well known, only eleven countries presently use robots in industry.

As more and more companies decide to incorporate robots into their organizations, robotics specialists will be needed to design and program the robots and to install them in the factories—in other words, to put those robots to work.

Along with mastering basic engineering skills, robotics specialists have to be mechanically **inclined** and creative, and know something about computer science.

Unlike other types of engineers, robotics specialists must be well **versed** in many areas. Designing a robot on a drawing board is only the first step. The real challenge is actually building it and putting it to work.

At the moment, most industrial robots work on assembly lines. But who can tell what this exciting new industry's future will bring?

Reprinted from *Real World,* with special permission of King Features Syndicate, Inc.

Choose from the story two words that are unfamiliar to you or whose meanings you are not completely sure of. (Do not choose words that appear in boldfaced type.) Write the words on the lines provided below. Then, beside each word, write what you think it means, based on how it was used in the story.

1. _____ : _____

   _____

2. _____ : _____

   _____

When you have finished the exercises in this lesson, go to your dictionary and find the definitions for the words you entered above. If a word has more than one meaning, look for the one that defines the word as it is used in the story. Then write the words and their dictionary definitions in the Student Words pages at the back of the book. How close did you come to figuring out their meanings for yourself?

3:1 Using Context

Below are five sentences from the reading passage. From the four answer choices that follow each sentence, choose the one that gives the best definition of the boldfaced word. Put an *x* in the box beside it. Use the context, or setting, provided by the sentence to help you discover the meaning of the word. If the sentence itself does not provide enough clues, go back to the passage and read the paragraph in which the sentence appears.

1. Two arms, capable of **executing** separate tasks at the same time, is one goal.
   - ☐ a. killing
   - ☐ b. imagining
   - ☐ c. botching up
   - ☐ d. carrying out

2. Beyond that, there is no telling just how complex these computer-operated helpers could **ultimately** become.
   - ☐ a. probably
   - ☐ b. without exception
   - ☐ c. in the end
   - ☐ d. possibly

3. Though robotics is a **relatively** new field, the demand for robotics experts will increase as more industries begin to see the potential applications for robots in their manufacturing operations.
   - ☐ a. somewhat
   - ☐ b. fundamentally
   - ☐ c. unquestionably
   - ☐ d. one of a kind

4. Along with mastering basic engineering skills, robotics specialists have to be mechanically **inclined** and creative, and know something about computer science.
   - ☐ a. operable
   - ☐ b. expert and experienced
   - ☐ c. having a tendency toward
   - ☐ d. ignorant

5. Unlike other types of engineers, robotics specialists must be well **versed** in many areas.
   - ☐ a. skilled or practiced
   - ☐ b. known or famous
   - ☐ c. secretly aware
   - ☐ d. summarized

3:2 Making Connections

In this exercise, the list of vocabulary words is followed by definitions of the words as they are used in the reading passage. Write each word in front of its definition.

execute   ultimately   relatively   inclined   versed

1. _____ : favorable or willing

2. _____ : carry out, do

3. _____ : to a degree, somewhat

4. _____ : experienced or skilled

5. _____ : in the end, finally

3:3 Making Connections

Below is a list of synonyms and antonyms for the five vocabulary words from this reading passage. On the lines provided, fill in the synonym and antonym for each vocabulary word.

finally   performing   completely   experienced   undoing

comparatively   uninterested   firstly   willing   ignorant

1. **executing**

   synonym: _____   antonym: _____

2. **ultimately**

   synonym: _____   antonym: _____

3. **relatively**

   synonym: _____   antonym: _____

4. **inclined**

   synonym: _____   antonym: _____

5. **versed**

   synonym: _____   antonym: _____

3:4 Making Connections

Complete each sentence with the correct vocabulary word.

executing   ultimately   relatively   inclined   versed

1. Roberta was not academically _____; she preferred doing things

   with her hands, such as building and repairing things.

2. Miguel knew all the theories behind aerodynamics, but _____ a flight

   was something he had not yet attempted.

3. After a hurried ten-minute pickup, Frieda's room was _____ clean, if

   not spotless.

4. The entire class was in awe of Jeanne, who had lived in Europe for ten years and was

   _____ in German, French and Italian, as well as in English.

5. No one ever learned what _____ happened to the hiking expedition

   that disappeared near the South Pole in 1872.

4: The Roots of Our Language

over- The prefix *over-* is one that you no doubt use all the time. It appears at the beginning of such common words as *overseas, overtime, oversleep, overnight* and *overhead.* If you think carefully about each of those words, you can probably figure out that *over-* carries the meanings above, across, too much, and extra, depending on the root word to which it is affixed. Let's look more carefully at some other words that begin with *over-*.

If you were to become a manager in an office, you would oversee the work of other employees. To oversee is to watch over or direct the activities of others. A person who supervises others is sometimes called an overseer, especially in the area of farm work. In factories, the person who oversees the work is usually called a supervisor, a foreman or a forewoman.

One thing that an overseer watches for is oversights. An oversight is an error made by accidentally leaving out, or overlooking, something. Something that is overlooked, of course, is not noticed. A person can make an oversight by leaving in something that doesn't belong, by leaving out something necessary, or by forgetting to do something. *The fact that I forgot to sign and date the form was an oversight, said Glen. I read the letter over pretty carefully, so I guess that spelling error was an oversight on my part.*

Someone who defends himself too strongly when explaining why he committed an oversight is overstating his case. People who express and defend their opinions too strongly are also guilty of overstatement. *Overstate* means to support too strongly. In other words, to say too much about something. An overstatement can also be an exaggeration: *I'll absolutely die if you don't let me go to the party!*

Sometimes people commit oversights on the job because they are overwhelmed by the amount of work they have to do. One meaning of overwhelmed is feeling unable to cope with a situation. Someone who says "It's all just too much! I can't deal with this!" is feeling overwhelmed. The
whelm root *whelm* means to cover up. So *overwhelm* is to cover up too much. The person who is piling all that work and pressure on the worker is overwhelming him or her. *Overwhelmed* can also mean to be overcome, or overpowered, by strong feelings, either good or bad. A person may be overwhelmed with sadness at the death of a pet, or overwhelmed with joy and excitement when given a surprise birthday party.

In addition to meaning too much to cope with or to bear, *overwhelming* can mean unexpectedly great, or far more than expected: *The democratic candidate won by an overwhelming majority of votes. The organization received an overwhelming response to its request for financial support.*

To end with a simple word, let's look at *overdress.* From our study of other words with the prefix *over-,* can you figure out what *overdress* means? It means either to dress too warmly or to dress too elaborately, too well, for an occasion. Someone who chose to wear an evening gown to a picnic would definitely be overdressed, as would someone who wore a down-filled parka in the tropics.

4:1 Write each word or root listed on the left beside its meaning on the right.

over-

oversight

overwhelm

oversee

overstate

1. _____ a mistake

2. _____ to overpower

3. _____ to exaggerate

4. _____ to direct or supervise

5. _____ above or higher than

4:2 Mark each statement as either true or false.

_____ 1. To overwhelm someone with your presence is to make her feel comfortable, even bored.

_____ 2. If you overstate your case, you state it in terms that are too strong—you exaggerate.

_____ 3. An oversight is a medical condition in which the afflicted cannot look down without becoming dizzy.

_____ 4. To oversee is to make a mistake, usually by accidentally leaving something out.

_____ 5. If you are overdressed, you are wearing clothes that are too fancy for the occasion.

4:3 Answer the following questions.

1. If you know that to be populated means to have people, what word do you think could be used to describe a place that has too many people? _____

2. Which word from the lesson means supervisor? _____

3. If *overexcited* means too excited, what word could be used to describe someone who is reacting too strongly to something? _____

4. If something is overhead, where is it? _____

5. Which word best describes how you would feel if one of your teachers assigned you to read three chapters in social studies in one night? _____

5: Extending Your Word Power

5:1 Multiple Meanings

Below are four vocabulary words that you met in this unit. Each has more than one meaning. Use the words to complete the sentences that follow. In those sentences the words have meanings that are different from those they had in the reading passages. If you are unsure of the various meanings of a word, look up the word in the glossary.

inclined   execute   offset   credit

1. The handsome movie star's deep blue eyes were _____ by the color of the sparkling ocean behind him.

2. Melanie took off her skis and _____ them against the side of the lodge.

3. The store would not give a cash refund, but they promised to _____ Mr. Donoff's account with the full amount he had paid for the defective swimming pool.

4. Eight soldiers had the misfortune to be chosen to _____ the convicted murderer.

5. Wheelchair ramps must be _____ at a shallow angle, for if they are built too steep they are difficult to maneuver in a wheelchair.

6. Janice did very well in the gymnastics competition, making her a real _____ to her coach.

7. The fun Greg anticipated having at the party _____ the work of preparing for it.

5:2 Roots Review

The incomplete sentences below contain words that you learned in the two roots lessons in this unit. Complete each sentence so that it makes sense and shows the meaning of the boldfaced vocabulary word.

1. Because the ship **submerged** quickly, the sailors on deck _____ _____ .

2. The large, well-kept **marina** attracted many _____ _____ .

3. The marching band that turned down the wrong street **detracted** _____ _____ .

4. "Mom," asked Edward, "could I please **subscribe** _____ _____ ?"

5. Because of an **oversight**, John's name _____ _____ .

6. By **overstating** his opinion, Will _____ _____ .

7. **Overwhelmed** by the sad news, Martha had to _____ _____ .

8. After surveying the other guests, James felt **overdressed**, so he _____ _____ .

9. "I'm sorry," said a shamefaced Mona. "I **retract** _____ _____ ."

10. Lisa's dream was to become a **mariner** because _____ _____ .

5:3 Choosing Just the Right Word

Some of the words you have worked with in this unit have synonyms. The synonyms have slightly different meanings from the vocabulary words.

Below are synonym studies for three of the vocabulary words. Use either the vocabulary words or their synonyms to complete the story that follows. Refer to the synonym studies as you decide which word carries the best meaning for each blank.

ultimate   final

Both of these words refer to something that follows all others. *Ultimate* means the last stage of a long process that could not possibly go any further. *Final* applies to a defined or planned end of a series or process.

interval   pause

These words define a limited period of time. An *interval* is space of time between two separate actions or events. A *pause* is a temporary stop in a continuing action.

versed   skilled

Both words have to do with knowledge and the ability to apply it. *Versed* means being familiarized with something by study or experience. To be *skilled* is to have mastered a technique through long experience.

Bridgette first tried to scale Mount Hood in June of 1978. During a brief

_____ early in the climb, she realized that her food supply would not

1

last more than halfway to the peak. She turned around, discouraged and defeated. Her second

expedition also ended in failure. Though her food supply was ample, Bridgette was unable to

find a passable route beyond the tree line.

At that point, Bridgette decided that in order to be successful, she would have to be better

_____ in the topography of the mountain and in the records of

2

previous climbers. After an _____ of six months devoted to those

3

studies, Bridgette was ready to try again. This would be her _____

4

attempt, for she felt that she couldn't be any better prepared. It was now or never. Already

_____ in the art of climbing, she hoped her detailed studies of the

5

mountain and of other people's experiences on it would give her the extra edge necessary to

reach the top—and _____ success.

6

This time Bridgette was determined to succeed. The trek was far from easy, but she felt strengthened by her newly acquired knowledge. As she approached the last stage of the climb, she knew she would become the first woman to reach the summit of Mount Hood.

5:4 Recognizing Other Word Forms

Each of the following sentences can be completed with other forms of the words you encountered in this unit. Those alternate forms are listed below in pairs. Write each pair of words in the blanks of the sentence the pair completes. Use what you learned about the vocabulary in the unit to help you figure out what the words mean.

credited / ultimate   **ultimatum / execution**

inclination / relation   **executed / agility**

versatility / offsetting

1. The _____ of the new kitchen gadget was amazing, _____ the minor disadvantages of its high price and complicated instructions for use.

2. The young acrobat _____ a double back flip with the _____ and grace of a ballerina.

3. Dr. Paulo was _____ with developing the _____ diet and exercise program for those with hearty appetites and unathletic natures.

4. Her mother gave Tina an _____ : either work on polishing her _____ of the piece she was to play for the recital, or give up piano lessons.

5. Samuel's strongest literary _____ was for murder mysteries, but the books he read varied in _____ to his mood.

5:5 Putting Your Vocabulary to Use

Use the vocabulary words from units five and six to complete the crossword puzzle.

ACROSS

1. thoroughly skilled
3. attribute; give praise
8. able to do many things well
10. fill with life and energy
11. ability to move quickly and easily
14. withdraw
15. highly able
16. one who carries things

DOWN

2. harbor
4. somewhat
5. place where one thing crosses another
6. sailor
7. an error made by not noticing something
9. docking area for small boats
12. lean toward
13. decide through reasoning
14. send money that is owed

GHOST

Looking for a good car game to help you pass the time on long drives? Here's one that's great fun for people who are pretty good spellers. You can play with as few as two players or as many as four or five.

The first player says a letter, and then all the players take turns adding letters that lead to the spelling of a word. (Alternate turns with two players, and go clockwise with three or more.) The object of the game, however, is to *avoid* giving a letter that completes a word. If, for instance, the getters *g, r, e* and *a* have been given, you do not want to say *t,* for that would complete the word *great.* Instead, you might add *s,* leading to *grease* or *greasy.* When a player gives a letter that ends a word, he or she gets one letter of the word *ghost*—a *g* the first time, an *h* the second time, and so on. A player who gets GHOST is out of the game.

Players must give letters that lead to real words. No one, however, says what word he or she has in mind when adding a letter. (So the next player might have a different word in mind and give a letter that leads to *that* word.)

The Challenge: If when it is your turn you can't think of a word that can be made by adding to the letters already given, you may try to bluff by saying just any letter. Be prepared, however, to be challenged.

If a player gives a letter that doesn't seem to be leading to a real word, the next player— and only the next player— may challenge by asking what word was being spelled. If the player who is challenged didn't have a real word in mind, he or she gets a letter of *ghost.* If a real word *was* being spelled, the person who issued the challenge gets the letter. A challenge must be made before another turn is taken. So if a number of players in a row bluff successfully, only the person who is finally challenged and caught gets a letter.

No proper nouns or common slang words are allowed.

Only words of at least four letters are counted against a player. So if the first few letters given in a round form such little words as *let* or *to,* those words do not count as completed words.

1:Meeting Words in Context

Reading Selection   Excerpt from *I Know Why the Caged Bird Sings* by Maya Angelou

Words Introduced   anticipation removed exerting secure excelled

2:The Roots of Our Language

Roots Introduced   mis-

3:Meeting Words in Context

Reading Selection   Excerpt from *The White Heron* by Sarah Orne Jewett

Words Introduced   demure rare snared acquaintances stolen

4:The Roots of Our Language

Roots Introduced   epi- demos -dermis

5:Extending Your Word Power

Multiple Meanings
Roots Review
Using Words Precisely
Recognizing Other Word Forms
Putting Your Vocabulary to Use

1:Meeting Words in Context

Excerpt from **I Know Why the Caged Bird Sings** by Maya Angelou

The children in Stamps trembled visibly with **anticipation**. Some adults were excited too, but to be certain the whole young population had come down with graduation epidemic. Large classes were graduating from both the grammar school and the high school. Even those who were years **removed** from their own day of glorious release were anxious to help with preparations as a kind of dry run. The junior students who were moving into the vacating classes' chairs were tradition-bound to show their talents for leadership and management. They strutted through the school and around the campus **exerting** pressure on the lower grades. Their authority was so new that occasionally if they pressed a little too hard it had to be overlooked. After all, next term was coming, and it never hurt a sixth grader to have a play sister in the eighth grade, or a tenth-year student to be able to call a twelfth grader Bubba. So all was endured in a spirit of shared understanding. But the graduating classes themselves were the nobility. Like travelers with exotic destinations on their minds, the graduates were remarkably forgetful. They came to school without their books, or tablets or even pencils. Volunteers fell over themselves to **secure** replacements for the missing equipment. When accepted, the willing workers might or might not be thanked, and it was of no importance to the pregraduation rites. Even teachers were respectful of the now quiet and aging seniors, and tended to speak to them, if not as equals, as beings only slightly lower than themselves. After tests were returned and grades given, the student body, which acted like an extended family, knew who did well, who **excelled**, and what piteous ones had failed.

Choose from the story two words that are unfamiliar to you or whose meanings you are not completely sure of. (Do not choose words that appear in boldfaced type.) Write the words on the lines provided below. Then, beside each word, write what you think it means, based on how it was used in the story.

1. _____ : _____

_____

2. _____ : _____

_____

When you have finished the exercises in this lesson, go to your dictionary and find the definitions for the words you entered above. If a word has more than one meaning, look for the one that defines the word as it is used in the story. Then write the words and their dictionary definitions in the Student Words pages at the back of the book. How close did you come to figuring out their meanings for yourself?

1:1 Using Context

Below are five sentences from the reading passage. From the four answer choices that follow each sentence, choose the one that gives the best definition of the boldfaced word. Put an *x* in the box beside it. Use the context, or setting, provided by the sentence to help you discover the meaning of the word. If the sentence itself does not provide enough clues, go back to the passage and read the paragraph in which the sentence appears.

1. The children in Stamps trembled visibly with **anticipation**.
   - ☐ a. fever and chills
   - ☐ b. nervousness and insecurity
   - ☐ c. excitement about what had just happened
   - ☐ d. excitement about what was to come

2. Even those who were years **removed** from their own day of glorious release were anxious to help with preparations as a kind of dry run.
   - ☐ a. absent
   - ☐ b. distant
   - ☐ c. taken away
   - ☐ d. beyond

3. They strutted through the school and around the campus **exerting** pressure on the lower grades.
   - ☐ a. hammering
   - ☐ b. eliminating
   - ☐ c. putting
   - ☐ d. relieving

4. Volunteers fell over themselves to **secure** replacements for the missing equipment.
   - ☐ a. build
   - ☐ b. fasten
   - ☐ c. get
   - ☐ d. get away with

5. After tests were returned and grades given, the student body, which acted like an extended family, knew who did well, who **excelled**, and what piteous ones had failed.
   - ☐ a. did moderately well
   - ☐ b. did exceptionally well
   - ☐ c. went too fast
   - ☐ d. were put out of school

1:2 Making Connections

Listed below are the five vocabulary words from the reading passage, followed by ten words and phrases that are related to them in some way. They may be synonyms, antonyms or definitions. On the line next to each word or phrase, write the vocabulary word that is related to it.

anticipation   removed   exerting   secure   excelled

1. get possession of _____

2. nearby _____

3. putting forth _____

4. failed _____

5. at a distance from _____

6. was superior _____

7. lack of interest _____

8. obtain _____

9. pulling back _____

10. expectation of what is to come

_____

1:3 Making Connections

Complete the following analogies by inserting one of the five vocabulary words in the blank at the end of each one. Remember that in an analogy the last two words or phrases must be related to each other in the same way that the first two are related.

anticipation　removed　exert　secure　excelled

1. short : brief : : distant : _____

2. trotted : galloped : : succeeded : _____

3. notice : ignore : : discard : _____

4. doubt : uncertainty : : eagerness : _____

5. support : encourage : : try : _____

1:4 Making Connections

Complete each sentence with the correct vocabulary word.

anticipation　removed　exerting　secure　excelled

1. When Patricia started baby-sitting, she found it difficult to control the children because she was not used to _____ her authority.

2. Because he did not celebrate Christmas, Mr. Kantor felt _____ from all the holiday preparations going on around him.

3. Carlos was not a very good tennis player, but he _____ in soccer.

4. In order to _____ a few pencils and some paper, Ms. Frank had to fill out request forms in duplicate and submit an up-to-date inventory of the entire English department's supplies.

5. The city's snowplows were put in top working order in _____ of the blizzard.

2: The Roots of Our Language

mis- The prefix *mis-* means the opposite of, the lack of, badly, or wrongly. It generally gives a root word an opposite meaning or a meaning that is negative. For example, *apprehend* means to understand the meaning of something. So a *misapprehension* (miss-ap-rih-HEN-shun) is a misunderstanding.

A way of saying that you figure out something is to say that you *calculate* it. You calculate things all the time in math class. But if you're having a bad day or your mind wanders, you may *miscalculate* (miss-KAL-kew-late), or figure incorrectly. Let's set up a very basic example. Say you add 8 plus 8 and get 17 as your answer. You would have miscalculated. In most such cases you will eventually realize you've made an error and correct it. But if for some reason you don't check your answer and discover that you've made a mistake, you may go on thinking that 8 plus 8 equals 17. You would be thinking that something is true when it's not. Then you would be suffering from a *misconception* (miss-kun-SEP-shun). A misconception is a wrong understanding of something. It applies to more than just math problems. You can have a misconception about ideas, theories or situations, as well.

One way we come by ideas is by *conceiving* (kun-SEEV-ing) them. To conceive means to take a thought into your mind. Naturally, if you can conceive, you can also *misconceive* (miss-kun-SEEV). To misconceive means to take a thought into your mind incorrectly. Usually when you misconceive it is because you've gotten off on the wrong foot. For example, if someone explains to you how to build a birdhouse, and you think the meaning of the carpentry term *to sand* is to fill something with sand, you won't correctly understand the explanation. So right at the start you will have misconceived the information, because you had an incorrect understanding of one of the main terms. As a result you may build a birdhouse that is fine in every way but one—it's filled with sand.

A word that is closely related to misconceive is *misconstrue* (miss-kun-STROO). The major difference between the two is that *misconstrue* has to do with not understanding someone's intentions rather than not understanding an idea or problem. To *construe* is to understand what someone means by what they say or by their actions. Let's set up another example. You and a casual friend are talking. Your friend says he likes your sweater, then laughs. Because of the laugh, you think he is being sarcastic. Later you find out that he laughed simply because he felt good and because he has a habit of laughing for no real reason—he's just a happy guy. He did genuinely like your sweater, but because of the laugh you misconstrued his meaning.

Now we've brought ourselves to a word that can be used as a synonym for both *misconceive* and *misconstrue*. The word is *misinterpret* (miss-un-TER-prut). Since *interpret* means to come to an understanding, it follows that *misinterpret* means to come to an incorrect understanding. *Misinterpret* could be used for *misconceive* in the birdhouse example. You could misinterpret the explanation. It could also be used for *misconstrue* in the sweater example. You could misinterpret your friend's laugh. You can misinterpret ideas as well as actions or words. And when you do, you come up with a *misinterpretation* (miss-un-TER-pruh-TAY-shun), or an incorrect understanding.

2:1 Write each word or root listed on the left beside its meaning on the right.

mis-

miscalculate

misconception

misconstrue

misinterpretation

1. _____ a wrong idea

2. _____ an error in judging or understanding

3. _____ to mistake the meaning of an action

4. _____ opposite or lack of; badly, wrongly

5. _____ to figure wrongly

2:2 Mark each statement as either true or false.

_____ 1. To add two plus two and come up with five is to miscalculate.

_____ 2. A misinterpretation is a total understanding of an idea or theory.

_____ 4. If someone pays you a false compliment in a sarcastic fashion but you think they are being sincere, you misconstrue their meaning.

_____ 4. A person who has the mistaken idea that the earth's crust and its core are the same thing has a misconception about the structure of the planet.

_____ 5. If you set off on a trip thinking it will take you twenty minutes, but it takes you five hours instead, you have miscalculated.

2:3 Answer the following questions.

1. If good conduct means proper behavior, what do you think *misconduct* means? _____

_____

2. You learned in the lesson that *apprehend* means to understand. What do you think *misapprehend* means? _____

_____

3. Keep in mind the prefix *mis-,* and make a word that means to put something in the wrong place.

_____

4. If you accidentally misdirect a person as to how to get to a certain place, that person will probably get _____ .

5. If a person makes a statement and you repeat that statement exactly as he said it, you *quote* him. What do you do if you fail to repeat the statement just as the person said it? _____

_____

3: Meeting Words in Context

Excerpt from **The White Heron** by Sarah Orne Jewett

"So Sylvy knows all about birds, does she?" he exlaimed, as he looked round at the little girl who sat, very **demure** but increasingly sleepy, in the moonlight. "I am making a collection of birds myself. I have been at it ever since I was a boy." (Mrs. Tilley smiled.) "There are two or three very **rare** ones I have been hunting for these five years. I mean to get them on my own ground if they can be found."

"Do you cage 'em up?" asked Mrs. Tilley doubtfully, in response to this enthusiastic announcement.

"Oh, no, they're stuffed and preserved, dozens and dozens of them," said the ornithologist, "and I have shot or **snared** every one myself. I caught a glimpse of a white heron three miles from here on Saturday, and I have followed it in this direction.

They have never been found in this district at all. The little white heron, it is," and he turned again to look at Sylvia with the hope of discovering that the rare bird was one of her **acquaintances**.

But Sylvia was watching a hop-toad in the narrow footpath.

"You would know the heron if you saw it," the stranger continued eagerly. "A queer tall white bird with soft feathers and long thin legs. And it would have a nest perhaps in the top of a high tree, made of sticks, something like a hawk's nest."

Sylvia's heart gave a wild beat; she knew that strange white bird, and had once **stolen** softly near where it stood in some bright green swamp grass, away over at the other side of the woods.

Choose from the story two words that are unfamiliar to you or whose meanings you are not completely sure of. (Do not choose words that appear in boldfaced type.) Write the words on the lines provided below. Then, beside each word, write what you think it means, based on how it was used in the story.

1. _____ : _____

   _____

2. _____ : _____

   _____

When you have finished the exercises in this lesson, go to your dictionary and find the definitions for the words you entered above. If a word has more than one meaning, look for the one that defines the word as it is used in the story. Then write the words and their dictionary definitions in the Student Words pages at the back of the book. How close did you come to figuring out their meanings for yourself?

3:1 Using Context
Put an *x* in the box beside each correct answer. For clues to the meanings of the words, reread the parts of the passage in which the words appear.

1. As used in the passage, **demure** means
   ☐ a. cowardly.
   ☐ b. brave.
   ☐ c. sad and upset.
   ☐ d. reserved and serious.

2. Birds that are **rare** are
   ☐ a. not often seen.
   ☐ b. not yet mature.
   ☐ c. difficult to catch.
   ☐ d. strange looking.

3. That the ornithologist **snared** birds means that he
   ☐ a. studied them for a long time.
   ☐ b. shot them with arrows.
   ☐ c. trapped them.
   ☐ d. stuffed and preserved them.

4. If the heron was one of Sylvia's **acquaintances**, that would indicate that
   ☐ a. she had tried to catch the bird.
   ☐ b. the bird was almost a pet to her.
   ☐ c. she had never seen the bird.
   ☐ d. she had seen the bird.

5. From the sentence in which **stolen** appears, you can tell that it means
   ☐ a. ran swiftly.
   ☐ b. took without asking.
   ☐ c. spoke very quietly so as not to be heard.
   ☐ d. moved very quietly so as not to be heard or seen.

3:2 Making Connections
In this exercise, the list of vocabulary words is followed by definitions of the words as they are used in the reading passage. Write each word in front of its definition. You will notice that the present tense *steal* is used in place of the past tense *stolen,* which appears in the passage.

demure   rare   snare   acquaintance   steal

1. _____ : person who is known but who is not a close friend

2. _____ : being or appearing to be modest, shy or serious

3. _____ : capture in a trap

4. _____ : move secretly or quietly

5. _____ : seldom seen or found

3:3 Making Connections

Write each vocabulary word on the line in front of the appropriate synonym and antonym. The present tense of *stolen, steal,* is used in this exercise.

demure   rare   snared   acquaintances   steal

		synonym	**antonym**
1.	_____	trapped	freed
2.	_____	reserved	bold
3.	_____	companions	strangers
4.	_____	uncommon	usual
5.	_____	creep	rush

3:4 Making Connections

The boldfaced words in the following sentences are short definitions or synonyms of the vocabulary words in the reading passage. On the line in front of each sentence, write the vocabulary word that has the same meaning as the boldfaced word or words.

demure   rare   snared   acquaintances   stole

1. _____ After three weeks, Jake finally **caught** the troublesome raccoon in a homemade trap.

2. _____ Lydia's behavior in her new school was **very quiet and reserved** until she got to know people better.

3. _____ On Thanksgiving night, when everyone else was asleep, Peter **crept quietly** downstairs and made himself a giant turkey sandwich.

4. _____ When Mrs. Mellion's botany class was on a field trip they came upon a purplish plant **seldom found** in the area.

5. _____ At the movies, Connie and Brian saw a group of **people they knew** from the neighborhood youth center.

4: The Roots of Our Language

epi- The prefix *epi-* means upon, near, or over. Perhaps you have seen the word *epicenter* (EP-ih-sent-er) in newspaper accounts of earthquakes. The epicenter is the area that is directly over the center of the earthquake. The center is deep in the earth where sections of the earth are moving against each other. As you might guess, the epicenter usually receives a great deal of damage.

demos While we're on the subject of catastrophes, let's look at *epidemic* (EP-uh-DEM-ik). The root *demos* means people, and, in this case, *epi-* means over. So *epidemic* means spreading over the people. The event most commonly associated with the word *epidemic* is the rapid spread of a contagious illness—influenza, for example. But anything that spreads rapidly over an area or among many people may be considered an epidemic. For instance, if everyone began wearing oven mittens all the time because a popular rock star did, that would be a fashion epidemic. A person who studies the causes of epidemic diseases and works to control their spread practices *epidemiology* (EP-uh-DEE-mee-AHL-uh-jee). Such a person is concerned only with those epidemics that involve sickness.

-dermis A word that looks quite like *epidemic* but that means something very different is *epidermis* (EP-uh-DER-mus). The epidermis is the outer layer of skin. As you know, *epi-* means over. *-Dermis* means skin. So the epidermis is the layer of skin that is over all the others. If you are having trouble with your epidermis, you need to consult a *dermatologist* (der-muh-TOL-uh-just). A dermatologist is a doctor who practices *dermatology* (der-muh-TOL-uh-jee)— the study and treatment of skin diseases.

It's time to get away from earthquakes, epidemics and epidermal problems. For a change of pace, let's look at the *epigraph* (EP-uh-graf). *Epi-* here is used in the sense of upon. *-Graph* means to write. An epigraph is an inscription engraved on something, often a building or a monument. It is usually a short saying, or, in the case of a monument, a poem or dedication. Epigraphs can also be found in many books, always at the beginning. In a book, an epigraph will be a quotation that hints at the book's theme.

An *epitaph* (EP-uh-taf) is similar to an epigraph, but more specialized. It is the writing engraved on a tomb or a gravestone. It is a brief statement in memory of the person who has died. Sometimes an epitaph will be a short poem describing the person, and some epitaphs are humorous. People who liked a good laugh while they were alive composed funny epitaphs for them-selves before they died. Of course, if one is thinking of having a funny epitaph, one must think carefully, because nothing pales so quickly as less-than-great humor, and an epitaph is going to be there a *long* time.

4:1 Write each word or root listed on the left beside its meaning on the right.

epi-

1. _____ a sickness that spreads rapidly among the people

epidemic

2. _____ an inscription on a tombstone

epidermis

3. _____ an inscription or motto on a building or in a book

epigraph

4. _____ on, over, around, or next to

epitaph

5. _____ outer layer of skin

4:2 Mark each statement as either true or false.

_____ 1. An epidemic is a sickness that affects only the outer layer of skin.

_____ 2. Epigraphs are written only for people who have died.

_____ 3. If you have freckles, or if you know someone who has freckles, those freckles are visible on the epidermis.

_____ 4. Cemeteries are full of epitaphs.

_____ 5. The bubonic plague that swept across Europe in the fourteenth century was a deadly epidermis.

4:3 Put an *x* in front of the answer choice you think is correct.

1. The part of the earth's surface that is directly above the center of an earthquake is called the

   □ a. epicenter.   □ b. epidemic.   □ c. epidermis.

2. A quotation from the Greek historian Herodotus in the front of a history book would be an

   □ a. epitaph.   □ b. epigraph.   □ c. epilogue.

3. A fashion craze that spreads rapidly, becoming a widespread fad, could be called a fashion

   □ a. epidemic.   □ b. epicenter.   □ c. epicycle.

4. If dermatology is the study and care of skin diseases, one who specializes in this branch of medicine is called a

   □ a. dermalogue.   □ b. dermatologist.   □ c. democracy.

5. Since *demos* means people, it stands to reason that an epidemic is a disease that sweeps across a wide area and affects many

   □ a. people.   □ b. epigrams.   □ c. dermatologists.

5:Extending Your Word Power

5:1 Multiple Meanings
Below are five vocabulary words that you met in this unit. Each has more than one meaning. Use the words to fill in the blanks in the sentences that follow. In those sentences the words have meanings that are different from the meanings they had in the passages you read. If you are unsure of the various meanings of a word, look it up in the glossary.

removed   secure   rare   snare   stolen

1. The campers rigged a _____ with which they hoped to catch the animal that was raiding their food supply.

2. By the time she got home from school Amelia had _____ almost all traces of the paint that Jordan had "accidentally" spilled on her hair in art class.

3. Mr. Hutchins took care to _____ all the doors and shutters, as well as the TV antenna on the roof, against the hurricane that was predicted.

4. When Gregory's new bicycle was _____ , he immediately suspected the gang of boys who had given him trouble on the street the previous week.

5. Beverly often forgot to order her steak _____ in a restaurant, and was disappointed when the meat arrived browner and drier than she liked it.

5:2 Roots Review
The incomplete sentences below contain words that you learned in the two roots lessons in this unit. Complete each sentence so that it makes sense and shows the meaning of the boldfaced vocabulary word.

1. The treasurer of the club announced that as a result of her **miscalculations** _____

_____

_____ .

2. In an effort to **apprehend** the terrorists, the police _____

_____ .

3. The **epigraph** indicated that _____

_____

_____ .

4. Myra, who **misconstrued** Frank's going to the pep rally alone, thought _____

_____ .

5. Since you've never spoken to me before, I had the **misconception** that _____

_____

_____ .

6. The newspapers began calling the large number of flu cases an **epidemic** when _____

_____ .

7. The **dermatology** textbook was filled with pictures of _____

_____ .

8. Since the first sign of the disease was a bluish discoloration of the **epidermis**, Karl got worried when

he noticed that _____

_____

_____ .

9. Oliver collects humorous **epitaphs** from _____

_____ .

10. When Jackie said that he didn't want to go to the movies with me on Saturday, I **misinterpreted**

that to mean that _____

_____ .

5:3 Choosing Just the Right Word

Many of the words you have worked with in this unit have a number of synonyms. The synonyms have slightly different meanings from the vocabulary words.

Below are synonym studies for three of the vocabulary words. Read them carefully. Then use either the vocabulary words or their synonyms to complete the exercise that follows. Use the synonym studies to help you decide which word carries the best meaning for the specific context of each sentence.

rare uncommon

Rare and *uncommon* can both be used to describe something that is not abundant or that does not happen often. *Uncommon* suggests something that is not often met or seen—something unusual. *She had an accent that was uncommon in those parts.* *Rare* suggests something highly uncommon and, in addition, often of high value because of its unusualness. *The archaeologists uncovered a rare Indian artifact.*

excel   exceed

Excel and *exceed* mean to go beyond a limit. *Exceed* implies going beyond a set limit or beyond what someone has achieved before. *Careful drivers do not exceed the speed limit. In the race, Tommy exceeded his own record. Excel* implies high quality or outstanding achievement. It may suggest being better than all others. *The twins excel in mathematics.*

catch   snare

Catch and *snare* both mean to possess or control by seizing. *Catch* implies the seizing of something that is in motion or in hiding. *Micky learned to catch fly balls. Snare* implies seizing by using a trap. *They hoped to snare several quails for dinner.*

1. Doug had not expected to _____ the football, but it landed directly in his hands.

2. The _____ gem would be valued at many thousands of dollars when properly cut and polished.

3. The boys crouched behind the bushes, hoping to see their homemade trap _____ a rabbit or a skunk.

4. Like their father, who is a national champion, Peter and Ben _____ in chess.

5. The small turrets and detailed woodwork around the doorways were _____ in a house built in the 1930s.

6. It isn't easy to _____ a playful cat that doesn't want to be taken indoors.

7. The beauty and grandeur of the Grand Canyon usually _____ the expectations of tourists.

8. Franklin Nurseries sells to people who are looking for the unusual, for they specialize in _____ plants imported from all over the globe.

9. In order to _____ his sales quota, Neil would have to sell an average of five hundred dollars worth of software equipment per week.

5:4 Recognizing Other Word Forms

Each of the following sentences can be completed with other forms of the words you encountered in the lessons in this unit. Those alternate forms are listed below in pairs. Complete each sentence with a word pair, writing each word in the correct blank. Use what you learned about the vocabulary in the unit to help you figure out what the words mean.

acquaint / security   **anticipatory / rarely**

demurely / steal   **removal / excellent**

exertion / snare

1. The mood of the crowd was _____ as they awaited the arrival of the legendary movie star who was _____ seen in public.

2. Only twelve hours after the _____ of his appendix, Michael's condition was listed as _____ .

3. Bonnie Sue greeted her father's guests _____ and then tried to _____ away as quickly as possible.

4. All members of the airplane crew were required to _____ themselves with the _____ precautions for turbulent weather and hijacking.

5. Worn out from the _____ of the chase, the bear was not sharp enough to avoid the _____ that had been set to trap him.

5:5 Putting Your Vocabulary to Use

This word-search puzzle contains seventeen vocabulary words from this unit or the last one. They are printed horizontally, vertically, diagonally, backward and upside down.

Begin by listing the vocabulary words next to their clues. Then find the words in the puzzle, circling them as you locate them.

1. _____ misunderstand

2. _____ get to know

3. _____ expectation

4. _____ trap

5. _____ seldom seen or found

6. _____ tombstone inscription

7. _____ modest and shy

8. _____ get; obtain

9. _____ sink below the surface

10. _____ root meaning write

11. _____ do especially well

12. _____ put forth

13. _____ root meaning people

14. _____ carry out, do

15. _____ exaggerate

16. _____ final offer or demand

17. _____ outer layer of skin

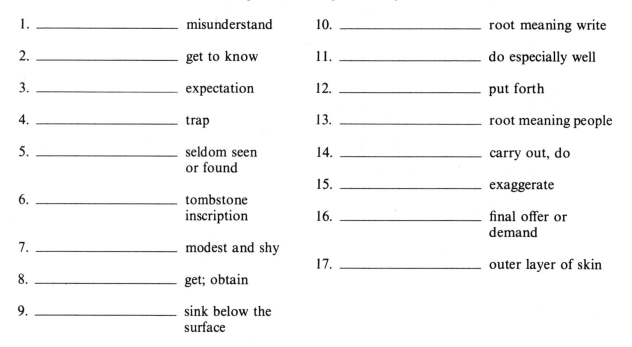

u	a	m	i	s	c	o	n	s	t	r	u	e
s	l	c	u	s	e	c	u	r	e	p	c	x
a	n	t	i	c	i	p	a	t	i	o	n	e
t	a	b	i	l	m	u	r	i	a	p	c	r
s	c	s	z	m	l	x	d	r	w	n	b	t
u	q	e	c	i	a	o	e	x	c	e	l	r
b	u	m	s	r	t	t	m	q	e	h	a	f
m	a	l	n	o	i	j	u	d	i	r	b	e
e	i	a	a	c	a	b	r	m	e	i	x	p
r	n	t	r	b	g	u	e	t	a	e	b	i
g	t	d	e	m	o	s	l	a	c	p	e	t
e	b	u	j	e	f	o	r	u	d	e	s	a
o	v	e	r	s	t	a	t	e	l	f	d	p
k	t	e	p	i	d	e	r	m	i	s	o	h

Windfalls

People have been thankful for windfalls for more than five hundred years. A windfall, as you probably are aware, is an unexpected gain or advantage—often a sum of money. The word *windfall* originally referred to trees that had been toppled by the wind. That meaning, too, is still alive. The figurative meaning came about in the sixteenth century. At that time, the English king and a few of his wealthy noblemen owned all the forests in the country. Because the landowners wanted to keep all the trees for themselves, the king proclaimed a law that made it illegal for peasants to fell a standing tree. This made things difficult for the peasants, who depended on wood as fuel for cooking and for heating their homes. Luckily, the king did allow peasants to carry away any trees that had been blown over by the wind. Though they couldn't count on when or where windfalls would occur, it was such fortunate accidents that allowed them to survive.

1: Meeting Words in Context

Reading Selection Shopping Tips

Words Introduced curb wary latter warp impartial

2: The Roots of Our Language

Roots Introduced ob- -ject inter- -ligate liter

3: Meeting Words in Context

Reading Selection It's Time to Get Yourself Organized

Words Introduced unique poses procrastinate strain efficient

4: The Roots of Our Language

Roots Introduced ab- dic solve duc

5: Extending Your Word Power

Multiple Meanings
Roots Review
Using Words Precisely
Recognizing Other Word Forms
Putting Your Vocabulary to Use

1: Meeting Words in Context

Shopping Tips

Know what you're buying! With the immense array of products on the market, being an intelligent consumer takes some work. But getting your money's worth is becoming easier all the time. It requires the investment of a little time and care, but in exchange you'll save money and grief. Here are some helpful hints:

Trial and error is absolutely the worst way to buy anything. Call it impulse buying, call it taking a chance on an unknown product, trial and error often leads to regret.

Advertising can't be ruled out as one way to gather product information, but you can trust it only so far. Although the Federal Trade Commission **curbs** some advertising abuses, it can't be everywhere. So learn what you can from those TV commercials, but take them with a grain of salt.

Past experience can tell you what products gave good service before. Still, a purchaser should understand that the quality of a product can change from year to year. So be **wary**, even with brands you think you know.

Comparison shopping is something you probably do already, within the limits of your time. You look in one store and then in another, comparing quality and price. A time not to comparison-shop is when a store has a really good sale and you know their bargains can't be beat. If they have what you want, buy it.

Word of mouth is a good way to learn about products. If several relatives and friends were pleased by a particular product, chances are you will be too.

The advice of experts can be helpful, but you usually have to be lucky enough to know someone whom you can trust to tell you the truth. A salesperson who is trying to sell you a particular product isn't a reliable expert.

Media reports—reports in newspapers and on radio and television—can be good sources of information.

Consumer publications are the best sources of product information. They include *Consumer Guide, Consumers' Research Magazine, Consumers Index* and *Consumer Reports*. The **latter** magazine is put out by Consumers Union, probably the most active nonprofit agency in the consumer field. CU is constantly buying products on the open market, testing them, and reporting on them. Consumer magazines do not accept advertising; it might **warp** their **impartial** judgment. They rate everything from air conditioners to yogurt.

Reprinted from *Real World,* with special permission of King Features Syndicate, Inc.

Choose from the story two words that are unfamiliar to you or whose meanings you are not completely sure of. (Do not choose words that appear in boldfaced type.) Write the words on the lines provided below. Then, beside each word, write what you think it means, based on how it was used in the story.

1. _____ : _____

_____

2. _____ : _____

_____

When you have finished the exercises in this lesson, go to your dictionary and find the definitions for the words you entered above. If a word has more than one meaning, look for the one that defines the word as it is used in the story. Then write the words and their dictionary definitions in the Student Words pages at the back of the book. How close did you come to figuring out their meanings for yourself?

1:1 Using Context

Write each vocabulary word beside its correct meaning. Try to figure out what the word means from the way it is used in the story.

1. curb

_____ make room for   _____ walk

_____ hold in check   _____ train

2. wary

_____ trusting   _____ on guard

_____ tired   _____ definite

3. latter

_____ last mentioned   _____ largest

_____ first   _____ best

4. warp

_____ offend   _____ cause to believe

_____ cause to judge   _____ disdain
              wrongly

5. impartial

_____ limited   _____ complete

_____ without basis   _____ showing no
                                                        favoritism

1:2 Making Connections

For each boldfaced vocabulary word in the sentences below, choose a synonym and an antonym from the list that follows. Write the synonyms and antonyms in the blanks.

clarify   increase   prejudiced   cautious   first

trusting   last   control   distort   unbiased

1. In order to **curb** her hunger until dinner time, Alison munched on an apple.

   synonym: _____   **antonym:** _____

2. Parents should warn their young children to be **wary** of strangers.

   synonym: _____   **antonym:** _____

3. After considering a blue, a purple and a red dress for the Christmas dance, Emily chose the **latter** because it was most in keeping with the holiday.

   synonym: _____   **antonym:** _____

4. Try not to let past disappointments **warp** your perception of new experiences.

synonym: _____ antonym: _____

5. When two of Everett's friends tried to get him to choose sides in an argument, Everett wisely chose to remain **impartial** and thereby keep both friends.

synonym: _____ antonym: _____

1:3 Making Connections
Complete the following analogies by inserting one of the five vocabulary words in the blank at the end of each one. Remember that in an analogy the last two words or phrases must be related to each other in the same way that the first two are related.

curb   wary   latter   warp   impartial

1. major : minor :: former : _____

2. audience : attentive :: jury : _____

3. furious : annoyed :: paranoid : _____

4. pull : tug :: twist : _____

5. construct : build :: restrain : _____

1:4 Making Connections
The boldfaced words in the following sentences are short definitions of or synonyms for the five vocabulary words you worked with in the last exercise. On the line in front of each sentence, write the vocabulary word that has the same meaning as the boldfaced word or words.

curb   wary   latter   warp   impartial

1. _____ John was afraid that his previous record of petty theft would **wrongly influence** the court's perspective on the current charges against him.

2. _____ Mary is trying to **control** her habit of criticizing people.

3. _____ Elizabeth and Donna both enjoyed drawing, but only the **second one** chose to submit her artwork for the annual street fair.

4. _____ There are few parents who can be **fair and unbiased** when it comes to their children's accomplishments.

5. _____ Young children should be taught to be **aware of possible danger** if a stranger approaches them on the street.

2: The Roots of Our Language

ob-   The prefix *ob-* has a few different meanings. It can mean toward, to, or against. Let's take the last meaning first and look at the word *object*. To object is to express an opinion against an idea or action. For instance, when a courtroom lawyer springs out of her chair and shouts, "I object, Your Honor," she is saying that she is against something, usually a question the other lawyer asked. She thinks that the question should be thrown out. To throw out is just about what the roots of *object* mean. As you will recall, the

-ject   root *-ject* comes from the Latin *jacere-,* meaning to throw.

inter-   Another word that makes use of the root *-ject* is *interject*. Since *inter-* means between, to interject means to throw between or into other things. If someone interrupts a conversation briefly to offer a fact or an opinion, they have interjected a comment.

But back to *ob-*. In the word *obligated, ob-* holds its second meaning: to. If you are obligated to do something, you are bound to do it by law or because you made a promise. The Latin root *-ligate* means to bind. So if you attach

-ligate   *ob-* to *-ligate,* you get "to bind." *-Ligate* can also be found in the word *ligament* (LIG-uh-munt). A ligament is a tough body tissue that connects bones or keeps organs inside the body in place. In other words, it binds, or holds, body parts.

liter   *Obliterate* is another *ob-* word in which the prefix means against. *Liter* comes from the Latin word *literra,* or letter. The root and the prefix combine to form a word that originally meant against the letters. So a written work that had been crossed out or blotted out so that it could no longer be read was said to have been obliterated. Eventually the word was applied more broadly, to mean to completely get rid of something.

In Unit 3 we encountered the *liter* root in the words *literate* (LIT-uh-rut), and *illiterate. Literate,* you will recall, means able to read and write. Someone who is illiterate cannot read or write. *Literate* has another meaning as well. It is used to refer to people who read or write on a high level. Such people are sometimes described as "well-read." Often such a person reads books and stories that make up literature. *Literature,* as you can see, begins with the root *liter.* Literature is writing that has lasting value because of its fineness of expression and the wide interest of the ideas it contains.

Let's return to *ob-* with a rather harsh word: *obnoxious* (ob-NOK-shus). A person who is obnoxious is disagreeable, annoying and generally not much fun to be around. You may have also come across obnoxious smells—from an industrial plant of some kind, for example. Sometimes those smells indicate poisonous or harmful gases, which are also called *noxious* (NOK-shus) gases. *Noxious,* then, means poisonous or harmful. *Ob-* combines with it to make *obnoxious,* meaning offensive, but not so offensive as to be poisonous.

Our next *ob-* word is *oblong,* which is an adjective that describes shape. Something that is oblong is longer than it is broad. A loaf of bread is oblong, as is an egg or something egg-shaped.

The last *ob-* words are *objectionable* and *objective*. Objectionable means disagreeable. It grows from the word *object*. Since to object is to disagree, an objection is a disagreement. It follows, then, that something objectionable is disagreeable or likely to cause objection. In the word *objective, ob-* means toward. An objective is a goal—something to move toward.

2:1 Write each word or root on the left beside its meaning on the right.

-ject

obligated

noxious

ob-

ligament

1. _____ toward, to or against

2. _____ a body tissue that connects bones

3. _____ harmful or poisonous

4. _____ bound by law

5. _____ throw

2:2 Mark each statement as either true or false.

_____ 1. The tissues connecting the bones in the human body are called ligaments.

_____ 2. A doctor uses a needle to interject medicine.

_____ 3. Usually when someone does you a favor you feel obligated to him.

_____ 4. When a noxious odor becomes strong enough, it may make you ill.

_____ 5. An oblong box has six unequal sides.

2:3 Put an *x* in front of the answer choice you think is correct.

1. A city destroyed by bombs has been
   ☐ a. obligated.   ☐ b. obliterated.   ☐ c. obstinate.

2. A person who constantly interrupts conversations with foolish remarks is
   ☐ a. obnoxious.   ☐ b. obligated.   ☐ c. obliterated.

3. When you speak against what someone else has said, you
   ☐ a. obtain.   ☐ b. oblong.   ☐ c. object.

4. A strong connecting body tissue is a
   ☐ a. literate.   ☐ b. lineament.   ☐ c. ligament.

5. A very bad-tasting substance might be
   ☐ a. noxious.   ☐ b. anxious.   ☐ c. notorious.

3: Meeting Words in Context

It's Time to Get Yourself Organized

Don't think you're **unique** if you find it hard to get down to work. Most people do. Part of the problem is taking that first step. Once you start working, it usually turns out not to be so bad, and you probably stay with the job until it is done.

For students, schoolwork often **poses** the greatest difficulties. You can take most of the pain out of getting started by organizing yourself. Here are some tips:

Organize your time

Try not to **procrastinate**. Start with the hardest tasks first. Then go on to the easier ones. If you leave the most difficult task for last, chances are you'll get to it when you're tired. There may not be enough time to do it properly. However, if you do it first, you'll probably breeze through the rest of your work.

Avoid last minute work

The quality of your work will be affected by leaving it to the last minute. Besides, why put yourself through all that unnecessary emotional strain? Plan your week ahead of time. On a Monday evening, take a long hard look at the week ahead. If a term paper is due on Friday and it requires a lot of research, start immediately, doing a little each night so that you're ready to write the paper on Thursday.

Avoid clutter

Keep your desk in order. Go through it each week and throw out what you don't need.

Mount a bulletin board over your desk

Keep important reminders and schedules on the board.

Keep a calendar

On it, list appointments, tests and events. When you complete a task or take a test, cross it off the calendar.

The schedules you set up should, of course, fit your own needs. The idea is to make your life easier, more manageable and more **efficient**.

Reprinted from *Real World*, with special permission of King Features Syndicate, Inc.

Choose from the story two words that are unfamiliar to you or whose meanings you are not completely sure of. (Do not choose words that appear in boldfaced type.) Write the words on the lines provided below. Then, beside each word, write what you think it means, based on how it was used in the story.

1. _____ : _____

   _____

2. _____ : _____

   _____

When you have finished the exercises in this lesson, go to your dictionary and find the definitions for the words you entered above. If a word has more than one meaning, look for the one that defines the word as it is used in the story. Then write the words and their dictionary definitions in the Student Words pages at the back of the book. How close did you come to figuring out their meanings for yourself?

3:1 Using Context

Put an *x* in the box beside each correct answer. For clues to the meanings of the words, reread the parts of the passage in which the words appear.

1. From the sentence following the one containing *unique,* you can tell that a **unique** person
   □ a. has a hard time working.
   □ b. is unorganized.
   □ c. is the same as everyone else.
   □ d. is unlike anyone else.

2. "Schoolwork **poses** difficulties for students" means that schoolwork
   □ a. eliminates difficulties.
   □ b. presents difficulties.
   □ c. takes the place of difficulties.
   □ d. makes up for difficulties.

3. The paragraph containing the word *procrastinate* and the paragraph following it are about the use of time. From the two paragraphs you can tell that **procrastinate** means to
   □ a. forget about work.
   □ b. do the hardest things first.
   □ c. do the easiest thing last.
   □ d. put off until later.

4. Emotional **strain** caused by having to worry about last minute work is
   □ a. emotional excitement.
   □ b. keeping a tight reign on emotions.
   □ c. pressure that wears on the emotions.
   □ d. not enough pressure to do good work.

5. An **efficient** life is one in which a person
   □ a. gets a lot done in a short time.
   □ b. doesn't have much to do.
   □ c. works all the time.
   □ d. has a busy schedule.

3:2 Making Connections

In this exercise, the list of vocabulary words is followed by definitions of the words as they are used in the reading passage. Write each word in front of its definition.

unique   poses   procrastinate   strain   efficient

1. _____ : productive without waste

2. _____ : presents or sets forth

3. _____ : severe pressure

4. _____ : one of a kind; having no equal

5. _____ : put things off until later

3:3 Making Connections

Write each vocabulary word on the line in front of the appropriate synonym and antonym.

unique   pose   procrastinate   strain   efficient

	synonym	antonym
1. _____	stress	ease
2. _____	unequaled	common
3. _____	delay	do
4. _____	productive	wasteful
5. _____	present	withdraw

3:4 Making Connections

Complete each sentence with the correct vocabulary word.

unique   poses   procrastinate   strain   efficient

1. The baby's sleeping schedule often _____ a problem when the Richard family goes on a long trip.

2. Even when a paper is assigned well in advance, it is Maria's habit to _____ about studying until the last minute.

3. Jules finished his chores in an _____ manner and still had time for a short bike ride before dinner.

4. The _____ of her father's illness left Franny without much energy to carry on her own life.

5. The new music had a fast, irregular rhythm and a _____ sound resembling a chorus of excited monkeys.

4: The Roots of Our Language

ab-
dic

The prefix *ab-* means away from. In the word *abdicate, ab-* combines with the Latin root *dic,* meaning to speak or proclaim. Perhaps you have seen the word *abdicate* used in connection with a king or a queen giving up power; the ruler abdicates the throne. You may wonder how *abdicate* came to mean give up or relinquish, since its roots don't seem to indicate such a definition. The answer lies in the fact that royal persons don't usually give up the throne without a little (or a lot) of pomp and circumstance. In other words, they make a big fuss and issue a formal statement in which they "proclaim" their intention of stepping "away from" the seat of power.

A more common word that uses the root *dic* is *dictate,* which means to speak or read aloud, or to command by giving orders. In both cases, the relation of the word's meaning to the root's meaning is clear: to dictate is to speak. From the second meaning of *dictate,* we get the word *dictator.* A dictator is a person who dictates, or speaks with absolute authority, as the ruler of a government. Dictators often take over governments by force, usually with the help of the army they command so absolutely. Needless to say, you won't catch many dictators abdicating their positions gracefully.

Let's look at some *ab-* words we've already touched on. *Absolute* comes from the Latin *absolvere,* which means set free, or absolve. The English word *absolve* means to set free, especially in the sense of freeing someone from guilt. *Absolute,* however, means total, complete or unquestioned. It first meant free from imperfection. That meaning led to the idea of being free from restrictions—complete and unquestioned. *Absolutely* means completely or totally. The dictator, for example, rules absolutely, and to be absolutely certain is to be totally certain.

Abstain, another word built on the root *ab-,* contains the Latin root *tenere,* meaning to hold. So *abstain* means to hold oneself away from something. A dieter (one with willpower anyway) abstains from fattening foods.

solve

We have already seen the root *solve* in *absolve.* It means to loosen. When you *solve* a problem, then, you "loosen" the elements of the problem the way you untie a knot. And a *solvent* is a substance that dissolves other substances—a kind of liquid problem solver.

Resolve is formed from the prefix *re-* and the root *solve.* It, too, means to solve a problem, but it carries the added idea of making a decision for a group of people. Someone who resolves an issue settles a question that is causing wide disagreement. A political issue, for example, gets resolved. *Resolve* also means to make a firm decision for oneself: *I resolve to get to bed early from now on.* And if you make that type of promise to yourself, you are making a *resolution.* Of course, a resolution is also what puts an end to that political issue we just discussed.

duc

To return to a word with the prefix *ab-,* let's examine *abduct.* It is made up of *ab-* plus the Latin root *duc,* meaning to lead. So *abduct* means to lead away from, usually by force. To kidnap someone, for example, is to abduct. If we add a *t* to *duc,* we get *duct*—a pipe or ditch that carries such things as air, water or gas. A duct leads such substances away from one place and to another, just as any good *duc* word should.

4:1 Write each word or root on the left beside its meaning on the right.

duct   1. _____ to hold oneself away from

abstain   2. _____ a substance that dissolves other substances

dictate   3. _____ an absolute ruler

solvent   4. _____ to command

dictator   5. _____ a pipe or channel

4:2 Mark each statement as either true or false.

_____ 1. Businessmen and women sometimes dictate letters to a secretary.

_____ 2. If you make a resolution, you are feeling uncertain.

_____ 3. One way for a queen to give up her duties is for her to abdicate.

_____ 4. A professional cleaner might use a solvent to remove a stain.

_____ 5. Voters often absolve from voting when they haven't made up their minds about a political issue.

4:3 Put an *x* in front of the answer choice you think is correct.

1. To free a man from punishment is to
   ☐ a. abdicate him.   ☐ b. resolve him.   ☐ c. absolve him.

2. The victim of a kidnapping has been
   ☐ a. abducted.   ☐ b. deducted.   ☐ c. inducted.

3. If you are allergic to nuts and someone offers you a cashew, you will probably
   ☐ a. retrain.   ☐ b. abstain.   ☐ c. restrain.

4. If the president of the stamp club decides she doesn't want to be president anymore, she might
   ☐ a. abstain.   ☐ b. resolve.   ☐ c. abdicate.

5. Someone who is inducted as a member of a club is
   ☐ a. abstained.   ☐ b. taken in.   ☐ c. expelled.

5: Extending Your Word Power

5:1 Multiple Meanings

Some of the vocabulary words from this unit have more than one meaning. Four of those words are listed below, together with their definitions. Use the words to complete the sentences that follow. In those sentences the words have meanings that are different from those they had in the reading passages.

curb

a. (v.) to hold in check; restrain

b. (n.) a border of concrete or stone along the edge of pavement

pose

a. (v.) to present or set forth

b. (v.) to hold or place in a certain position

strain

a. (n.) trying or wearing pressure

b. (n.) physical force or weight that stretches

c. (v.) to injure by too much effort or stretching

warp

a. (v.) to distort; lead or turn from good to bad

b. (v.) to bend or twist out of shape

1. The seventeen inches of snow deposited by the blizzard put a _____ on the old house's weak roof.

2. Main Street has been resurfaced several times over the years, but it still retains the original stone _____ , complete with hitching posts, that was installed over a century ago.

3. Dino wrapped his paintings carefully and put them in a leather portfolio so that the humidity would not _____ the canvases.

4. The _____ on Belle's weak ankle was too much; she sat by the side of the road and waited for a passing farmer to offer her a ride.

5. The art teacher asked Max to _____ for the fifth-period portrait class.

6. David carelessly placed a record album on the gas heater, forgetting that the

   heat would _____ the plastic disc.

5:2 Roots Review
The incomplete sentences below contain words that you learned in the two roots lessons in this unit. Complete each sentence so that it makes sense and shows the meaning of the boldfaced vocabulary word.

1. The townspeople **objected** to the new traffic light because _____

   _____ .

2. When it came to helping out around the house, Sarah felt **obligated** _____

   _____ .

3. Because of a torn **ligament**, Central High's ace quarterback _____

   _____ .

4. Having been exposed to the **noxious** fumes for hours, the workmen _____

   _____ .

5. The captain shouted over the desert wind, "Step lively, people, our **objective** _____

   _____ ."

6. Jerry decided to **abdicate** the _____

   _____ .

7. The **dictator** responded to all criticism by _____

   _____ .

8. When Theodore mistakenly applied the **solvent** _____

   _____ .

9. Carrie **resolved** _____

   _____ .

10. When the president of Kingsfield Industries was **abducted** _____

   _____ .

5:3 Choosing Just the Right Word

Many of the words you have worked with in this unit have a number of synonyms. As you know, in some cases the synonyms have slightly different meanings from the vocabulary words.

Following are synonym studies for three of the vocabulary words. Use either the vocabulary words or their synonyms to complete the sentences in the exercise that follows. Refer to the synonym studies as you decide which choice carries the best meaning for the specific context of each sentence.

cautious   wary

Cautious and *wary* both mean watchful in situations that are dangerous or risky. *Cautious* implies that care has been taken to be safe. It means taking no chances. *Ronald was cautious when riding his bike at night.* *Wary* emphasizes suspiciousness and alertness—watching for danger or risk. *Kate was advised to be wary of her new neighbors.*

delay   procrastinate

Delay and *procrastinate* both mean to move or act slowly so as to fall behind schedule. *Delay* usually implies holding back from doing or finishing something because of interference of some sort. *Helen's flight was delayed because of bad weather.* *Proscrastinate* implies putting off on purpose, out of laziness or lack of interest, something that needs to be done. *Anne hated housework, so she procrastinated about cleaning her room until it was an absolute mess.*

effective   efficient

Effective and *efficient* both have to do with the ability to produce a result. *Effective* stresses the actual production or the power to produce a result. *Salk discovered a vaccine effective in preventing polio.* *Efficient* suggests functioning as well as possible without wasting energy. *A small car is more efficient than a large one.*

1. Jake had to _____ dinner for an hour because his father had to work overtime.

2. When Sergio decided to earn money by shoveling snow from driveways, he bought himself the biggest snow shovel he could comfortably handle, so as to do the job in the most _____ way possible.

3. Having been bitten by a huge German shepherd when he was only three, Mike was _____ of all dogs.

4. His mother's threat to ground Jason for a week if he didn't do all his chores proved an _____ way of getting him to tend to his responsibilities.

5. Doreen was exasperated with her tendency to _____ about schoolwork, and swore to do all her work promptly starting the next term.

6. It pays to be especially _____ when driving on a holiday weekend.

5:4 Recognizing Word Forms

The words listed below are other forms of the vocabulary words you have worked with in this unit. Fill in the blank in each sentence with the correct vocabulary word. Use what you have learned in this unit to help you figure out what the words mean. If you are unsure of the meaning of a word, look the word up in the glossary.

impartiality   posing   uniqueness   efficiency   procrastination   wariness

1. Peter was surprised at the _____ with which his little sister prepared dinner.

2. The _____ of the umpire is essential to a fair game of baseball.

3. After _____ the problem to the class, Mr. Gurney waited for suggestions for a solution.

4. Adam's constant _____ causes him real problems, for when he finally does his work, at the last possible moment and in a hurry, he naturally does a poor job.

5. The _____ of the new playground lay in the fact that the children themselves had designed and built it.

6. Seth's _____ of the older, tough-looking kids in his neighborhood kept him from joining the afternoon games of touch football in the empty lot.

5:5 Putting Your Vocabulary to Use

The scrambled words below are all vocabulary words from this unit or the last one. Use the definition or synonym next to each scramble to help you figure out what the word is. Then write the word in the space provided. The number of lines in each answer space also provides a clue to the word. The circled letters will form a phrase related to consumers and shopping. Write that phrase on the line at the bottom of the puzzle.

1. EEFTNIIFC   able to produce without waste of time or energy

2. PAWR   distort

3. REBLAETOIT   wipe out

4. USRBC   controls

5. NIERTPRTE   explain the meaning of

6. TNISBAA   hold oneself back from

7. CDTU   ditch that carries air, gas or water

8. VCEOEJBTI   aim or goal

9. EOPS   body position

10. ECRROPSAAITNT   put off until later

11. LTSOE   moved secretly or quietly

12. UXONSOI   physically harmful

13. TINASR   great pressure

14. HIGPEARP   inscription in a book

15. MTERUSOCISN   misunderstand

16. GMILTNEA   strong body tissue that connects bones

1. _ O _ _ _ _ _

2. _ O _ _

3. _ _ _ O _ _ _ _ _ _

4. _ _ _ _ O

5. _ _ _ O _ _ _ _

6. O _ _ _ _ _ _

7. O _ _ _

8. _ _ _ _ _ _ _ O _

9. _ _ _ O

10. _ O _ _ _ _ _ _ _ _

11. _ O _ _ _

12. _ _ _ O _ _ _

13. O _ _ _ _ _

14. _ _ O _ _ _ _ _

15. _ _ _ _ _ O _ _ _ _

16. _ _ O _ _ _ _ _

Phrase: _____

UNIT 9

1: Meeting Words in Context

Reading Selection   Abraham Lincoln's *Gettysburg Address*

Words Introduced   conceived   proposition   consecrate   detract resolve

2: The Roots of Our Language

Roots Introduced   hyper-

3: Meeting Words in Context

Reading Selection   *Solitude* by Henry David Thoreau

Words Introduced   imbibes   congenial   burden   wholesome solitude

4: The Roots of Our Language

Roots Introduced   pro-   vide   -test

5: Extending Your Word Power

Multiple Meanings
Roots Review
Using Words Precisely
Recognizing Other Word Forms
Putting Your Vocabulary to Use

1: Meeting Words in Context

Abraham Lincoln's **Gettysburg Address**

Four score and seven years ago our fathers brought forth on this continent, a new nation, **conceived** in Liberty, and dedicated to the **proposition** that all men are created equal.

Now we are engaged in a great civil war; testing whether that nation, or any nation so conceived and so dedicated, can long endure. We are met on a great battlefield of that war. We have come to dedicate a portion of that field as a final resting-place for those who here gave their lives that that nation might live. It is altogether fitting and proper that we should do this.

But, in a larger sense, we cannot dedicate—we cannot **consecrate**—we cannot hallow—this ground. The brave men, living and dead, who struggled here have consecrated it far above our poor power to add or **detract**. The world will little note, nor long remember, what we say here, but it can never forget what they did here. It is for us the living, rather, to be dedicated here to the unfinished work which they who fought here have thus far so nobly advanced. It is rather for us to be here dedicated to the great task remaining before us—that from these honored dead we take increased devotion to that cause for which they gave the last full measure of devotion; that we here highly **resolve** that these dead shall not have died in vain; that this nation, under God, shall have a new birth of freedom; and that government of the people, by the people, for the people, shall not perish from the earth.

Choose from the story two words that are unfamiliar to you or whose meanings you are not completely sure of. (Do not choose words that appear in boldfaced type.) Write the words on the lines provided below. Then, beside each word, write what you think it means, based on how it was used in the story.

1. _____ : _____

  _____

2. _____ : _____

  _____

When you have finished the exercises in this lesson, go to your dictionary and find the definitions for the words you entered above. If a word has more than one meaning, look for the one that defines the word as it is used in the story. Then write the words and their dictionary definitions in the Student Words pages at the back of the book. How close did you come to figuring out their meanings for yourself?

1:1 Using Context

Put an x in the box beside each correct answer. For clues to the meanings of the words, reread the parts of the passage in which the words appear.

1. To be **"conceived** in Liberty" is to be
   ☐ a. planned with liberty as the foundation.
   ☐ b. regarded as being free.
   ☐ c. allowed to have liberty under certain conditions.
   ☐ d. planned to include liberty some time in the future.

2. Since we are told that "all men are created equal" is a proposition, a **proposition** must be a
   ☐ a. statement of fact.
   ☐ b. motion brought up for a vote.
   ☐ c. statement of belief.
   ☐ d. question presented for consideration.

3. To **consecrate** ground means to
   ☐ a. fight a battle on it.
   ☐ b. declare it sacred—worthy of great respect.
   ☐ c. prepare it for building.
   ☐ d. use it for religious services.

4. From the last few words of the sentence in which **detract** appears, we can guess that the word means to
   ☐ a. eliminate.
   ☐ b. add on.
   ☐ c. take away.
   ☐ d. intrude.

5. To **resolve** that the dead shall not have died in vain is to
   ☐ a. firmly decide that they will not have died senselessly.
   ☐ b. try to believe that they have died for a good cause.
   ☐ c. overlook the fact that they have died.
   ☐ d. disregard the fact that death has taken place.

1:2 Making Connections

In this exercise, the list of vocabulary words is followed by definitions of the words as they are used in the reading passage. Write each word in front of its definition.

To figure out what each word means, go back to the passage and read the sentence that contains the word. If you can't discover the meaning from the way the word is used in the sentence, read the sentences that come before and after it for clues.

conceived   proposition   consecrate   detract   resolve

1. _____ : take away a part; remove some of the quality or worth

2. _____ : formed in the mind; thought up

3. _____ : determine or decide; make up one's mind

4. _____ : statement presented

5. _____ : set aside as worthy of deep respect

1:3 Making Connections

Below, the five vocabulary words are followed by ten words or phrases that are related to them in some way. The ten words or phrases may be synonyms, antonyms or definitions. On the line next to each word or phrase, write the vocabulary word that is related to it.

conceive   proposition   consecrate   detract   resolve

1. diminish _____   6. statement _____

2. originate _____   7. make special _____

3. dedicate _____   8. determine _____

4. improve _____   9. imagine _____

5. be uncertain _____   10. idea _____

1:4 Making Connections

Complete each sentence with the correct vocabulary word.

conceived   proposition   consecrated   detract   resolve

1. The people honored traditions that had been _____ by time and generations of followers.

2. Every New Year's Eve, Dorothy and her brother, Kirk, _____ to stop fighting with each other, but the peace lasts only a day or two.

3. The Brookes Jr. High School Debating Team was founded on the _____ that all people love to argue.

4. Charles hoped that the small rust spot over one of the wheels of his Stingray would not _____ from the overall attractiveness of the car.

5. Joan and her classmates in psychology _____ a plan that would give them more time to devise their own experiments.

2: The Roots of Our Language

hyper-   To say that the prefix *hyper-* means over is correct, but it is too simple. *Hyper-* does come from the Greek root meaning over, but it has now taken on additional meanings—super and excess, for instance. A person who is hypersensitive (HY-per-SEN-sut-iv) might also be described as being super-sensitive, or sensitive to an abnormal degree. And a person who is hyperactive (HY-puh-RAK-tiv) is so excessively active that some sort of medical treatment may be called for. Likewise, *hyperacidity* (HY-puh-ruh-SID-ut-ee) is the condition of having too much acid in the stomach, the result being a painful burning sensation.

Anyone who uses wild exaggeration is indulging in *hyperbole* (hy-PER-buh-lee). To describe a crook as having a police record "a mile long" is to use hyperbole. Hyperbole has its place, of course; it is often used in humor. But if you're trying to get the straight facts across to someone, it's best to do so without *hyperbolizing,* which means, naturally, exaggerating.

Until now we've been looking at *hyper-* the prefix. As you have seen, it's quite a common prefix—so common, in fact, that over time it has become a word in and of itself. The word *hyper* is short for *hyperactive,* which we discussed at the beginning of the lesson. You may already be in the habit of using *hyper,* or you may have heard someone else use it. If so, you know that a person described as being hyper is high-strung and excitable. Usually a hyper person is filled with an excess of nervous energy, and is incapable of sitting still for very long.

Getting back to the prefix *hyper-,* we have *hypercritical* (HY-per-KRIT-ih-kul), which means overly critical. A critical person tends to find fault and point it out. That tendency is often a positive one, for it can mean seeing a thing clearly in order to judge it fairly. Being hypercritical, on the other hand, means judging other people or things by standards that are too strict—standards that cannot be met.

Most of the words we have examined so far have rather negative meanings, but such is not the case with all *hyper-* words. For example, the opposite of amnesia, which is the loss of memory, is hypermnesia (hy-perm-NEE-zhuh). That describes having unusually vivid or complete recall of past events—in short, a great memory. And hypersonic (HY-per-SAHN-ik) speed is five times faster than the speed of sound, which is 760 miles per hour. A hypersonic vehicle would come in pretty handy if you needed to get someplace in a hurry. Also, the state of being plain old hyper isn't bad if it's under control. A hyper person can get a lot done.

Finally, here's a *hyper-* word that is neither negative nor positive—just weird. Hyperspace is space of more than three dimensions or a dimension other than the three dimensions, length, width and height, that we are used to dealing with. In other words, it's not outer space, it's *other* space—one that scientists are not even sure exists. Science fiction writers are sure it exists, though; their characters come and go from hyperspace like it's the corner drugstore. Are the writers right? Does it exist? Do you need a hypersonic vehicle to reach it? Time will tell.

2:1 Write each word or root listed on the left beside its meaning on the right.

hyper-

hypersonic

hyperactive

hyperbole

hypermnesia

1. _____ exaggerated expression

2. _____ five times faster than the speed of sound

3. _____ extremely good memory

4. _____ over, super

5. _____ overly active

2:2 Mark each statement as either true or false.

_____ 1. The area deep in space beyond Pluto, where comets come from, is called hyperspace.

_____ 2. Speaking in glowing terms about the good qualities of a friend is called hyperbole.

_____ 3. Hyperactive people might have trouble sitting through a long movie.

_____ 4. Someone with hypermnesia cannot recall anything from his or her past.

_____ 5. An actor or an actress would probably not want to appear before a hypercritical audience.

2:3 Answer the following questions.

1. Why can't astronauts travel into hyperspace? _____

_____

2. Would you expect to find hyperbole in a politician's campaign speech? _____

_____

3. If you had hypermnesia, what would you be able to do that most other people can't? _____

_____

4. Why wouldn't a hyperactive person make a good space shuttle crew member? _____

_____

_____

5. What is another term for being greatly disturbed by things that don't have a strong effect on others?

_____ _____

3: Meeting Words in Context

Solitude by Henry David Thoreau

This is a delicious evening, when the whole body is one sense, and **imbibes** delight through every pore. I go and come with a strange liberty in Nature, a part of herself. As I walk along the stony shore of the pond in my shirt sleeves, though it is cool as well as cloudy and windy . . . all the elements are unusually **congenial** to me. The bullfrogs trump to usher in the night, and the note of the whippoorwill is borne on the rippling wind from over the water.

While I enjoy the friendship of the seasons I trust that nothing can make life a **burden** to me. The gentle rain which waters my beans and keeps me in the house today is not drear and melancholy, but good for me too. Though it prevents my hoeing them, it is of far more worth than my hoeing. . . .

My nearest neighbor is a mile distant, and no house is visible from any place but the hilltops within half a mile of my own. I have my horizon bounded by woods all to myself; a distant view of the railroad where it touches the pond on the one hand, and of the fence which skirts the woodland road on the other.

But for the most part it is as solitary where I live as on the prairies. It is as much Asia or Africa as New England. I have, as it were, my own sun and moon and stars, and a little world all to myself. . . .

I find it **wholesome** to be alone the greater part of the time. To be in company, even with the best, is soon wearisome and dissipating. I love to be alone. I never found the companion that was so companionable as **solitude**.

Choose from the story two words that are unfamiliar to you or whose meanings you are not completely sure of. (Do not choose words that appear in boldfaced type.) Write the words on the lines provided below. Then, beside each word, write what you think it means, based on how it was used in the story.

1. _____ : _____

   _____

2. _____ : _____

   _____

When you have finished the exercises in this lesson, go to your dictionary and find the definitions for the words you entered above. If a word has more than one meaning, look for the one that defines the word as it is used in the story. Then write the words and their dictionary definitions in the Student Words pages at the back of the book. How close did you come to figuring out their meanings for yourself?

3:1 Using Context
Below are five sentences from the reading passage. From the four answer choices that follow each sentence, choose the one that gives the best definition of the boldfaced word. Put an *x* in the box beside it. Use the context, or setting, provided by the sentence to help you discover the meaning of the word. If the sentence itself does not provide enough clues, go back to the passage and read the paragraph in which the sentence appears.

1. This is a delicious evening, when the whole body is one sense, and **imbibes** delight through every pore.
   - ☐ a. creates
   - ☐ b. announces
   - ☐ c. takes in
   - ☐ d. offers up

2. As I walk along the stony shore of the pond in my shirt sleeves, though it is cool as well as cloudy and windy . . . all the elements are unusually **congenial** to me.
   - ☐ a. rich
   - ☐ b. agreeable
   - ☐ c. warm
   - ☐ d. upsetting

3. While I enjoy the friendship of the seasons I trust that nothing can make life a **burden** to me.
   - ☐ a. puzzle
   - ☐ b. friend
   - ☐ c. pleasure
   - ☐ d. heavy load

4. I find it **wholesome** to be alone the greater part of the time.
   - ☐ a. homey
   - ☐ b. lonely
   - ☐ c. beneficial
   - ☐ d. difficult

5. I never found the companion that was so companionable as **solitude**.
   - ☐ a. being alone
   - ☐ b. calm and quiet
   - ☐ c. good company
   - ☐ d. nature

3:2 Making Connections
Complete the following analogies by inserting one of the five vocabulary words in the blank at the end of each one. Remember that in an analogy the last two words or phrases must be related in the same way that the first two are related.

imbibe   congenial   burden   wholesome   solitude

1. fun : game : : heavy : _____

2. group : companionship : : individual : _____

3. depressing : joyful : : unhealthy : _____

4. see : observe : : drink in : _____

5. disgusting : unappealing : : pleasant : _____

3:3 Making Connections

Below is a list of synonyms and antonyms for the five vocabulary words from this reading passage. On the lines provided, fill in the synonym and antonym for each vocabulary word.

unsuitable   absorb   load   emit   help

beneficial   aloneness   agreeable   companionship   unhealthy

1. **imbibe**

   synonym: _____   antonym: _____

2. **congenial**

   synonym: _____   antonym: _____

3. **burden**

   synonym: _____   antonym: _____

4. **wholesome**

   synonym: _____   antonym: _____

5. **solitude**

   synonym: _____   antonym: _____

3:4 Making Connections

The boldfaced words in the following sentences are short definitions of or synonyms for the five vocabulary words you worked with in the last exercise. On the line in front of each sentence, write the vocabulary word that has the same meaning as the boldfaced word or words.

1. _____ Though she was nervous about being in a new school where she did not know anyone, with a little effort and a ready smile Monica soon found a group of **friendly and agreeable** people to spend time with.

2. _____ An only child, Simon was accustomed to **being alone**.

3. _____ The MacDonald family loves the beach; they like to bodysurf in the crashing waves, lie on the hot sand, and **take in** the fresh salt air.

4. _____ Ruth became interested in cooking at an early age, and by the time she was eleven she was able to prepare delicious, **healthful** meals for the family.

5. _____ Mr. Caldwell made it clear that until the guilty party confessed, the entire class would carry the **weight** of responsibility for the missing posters.

4: The Roots of Our Language

pro-

We have already covered the prefix *pre-,* which means forward, before or in favor of. Now we have the prefix *pro-,* which means just the same things. Why does our language need two prefixes that have the same meaning? The answer is that much of our language comes from Greek and from Latin. Greek gave us *pro-,* and Latin gave us *pre-.*

A good example of a *pro-* word is *produce,* which means to make something or cause it to appear. In an earlier lesson you learned that the root *duc* means to lead. Produce, then, means to put something forward, as you do when you make something or when you cause something to appear. When you make something, you are that object's producer. Produce can also be a noun. Fruits and vegetables are called produce (PRO-doos); they are what farmers have produced.

A proponent is one who is in favor of something. In this word *pro-* combines with a root meaning to put or place, to make a word that means someone who takes a stand, or places himself, in favor of something. A proponent's natural enemy is his opponent, or one who takes a stand against something.

Proclaim (pro-KLAME), another word using *pro-* as a prefix, means to make a declaration or a demand publicly. The act of proclaiming results in a *proclamation* (PROK-luh-MAY-shun), which is a formal statement expressing the idea being proclaimed. Abraham Lincoln's *Emancipation Proclamation* was a formal statement expressing the idea that the Confederacy's slaves were to be freed.

vide

Many *pro-* words have more in common than just their shared prefix. Another root forms a link, as well. *Provide* (pruh-VIDE) means to prepare for a future need. The Latin root *vide* means to see, which is how the idea of the future came to be built into *provide.* It means literally to see forward. *Provident* (PRAHV-ud-unt) also holds the idea of a time to come, for it means making careful plans for the future. A provident person is one who plans ahead. *Providence* (PRAHV-ud-unts), as you might imagine, means the quality of being provident. It also has a bigger meaning, that of divine guidance. When it is spelled with a capital *P,* it refers to a watchful God who offers divine guidance. Since we're still on planning ahead, *provision* (pruh-VIZH-un) means to supply with food and materials. When you provision a ship, you put supplies on board for the long trip ahead; naturally, those supplies are called provisions.

If you've ever tried to produce a response or an action in someone, you will be interested in *provoke,* because that's what it means. If you taunt someone until they want to hit you, you are provoking a fight. This is not recommended. Provoking laughter is a much safer pastime, and all you have to do is tell a joke.

-test

Our last *pro-* word is *protest.* The root *-test* means to witness or testify. Therefore, to protest means to testify, or state, that you object to something. In the Vietnam era, antiwar demonstrators testified in the streets against an unpopular war. They generally tried to protest within sight of, or before, government buildings, which they saw as being symbolic of the government's foreign policy. And when they demonstrated, they issued a statement of disagreement, or a *protest.*

4:1 Write each word or root on the left beside its meaning on the right.

proclaim

1. _____ divine guidance or care

proponent

2. _____ before, in favor of

providence

3. _____ something prepared

pro-

4. _____ someone in favor of something

provision

5. _____ to declare publicly

4:2 Mark each statement as either true or false.

_____ 1. In order to practice for an important test, students sometimes take a protest.

_____ 2. State governors sometimes issue proclamations to honor important people and events.

_____ 3. It's usually better to work toward an agreement than to provoke an argument.

_____ 4. To make provisions for winter means to plan a vacation to escape the cold weather.

_____ 5. A provident person is practical.

4:3 Put an *x* in front of the answer choice you think is correct.

1. When a bill is introduced in Congress, those in favor of it are

☐ a. proponents.   ☐ b. opponents.   ☐ c. proposers.

2. People who feel they have been given some sort of divine guidance or help give their thanks to

☐ a. provident.   ☐ b. prominent.   ☐ c. Providence.

3. Another word for a stock of supplies or food is

☐ a. provinces.   ☐ b. provisions.   ☐ c. permissions.

4. A public announcement is a

☐ a. provocation.   ☐ b. proclamation.   ☐ c. production.

5. To make strong objections to something is to

☐ a. protest.   ☐ b. pretest.   ☐ c. provoke.

5: Extending Your Word Power

5:1 Multiple Meanings
Some of the vocabulary words you met in this unit have more than one meaning. Five words and their definitions are listed below. In the sentences that follow, fill in the blanks with the correct vocabulary words. To determine which word belongs in each sentence, refer to the definitions that are given.

conceive

a. (v.) to form in the mind; think up

b. (v.) to become pregnant with

proposition

a. (n.) a statement presented as fact

b. (n.) something presented for consideration or acceptance; a proposal

imbibe

a. (v.) to absorb

b. (v.) to drink

consecrate

a. (v.) to devote to a purpose; dedicate

b. (v.) to swear into permanent office with a religious rite

burden

a. (n.) something carried; a heavy weight or load

b. (v.) to impose a heavy weight or load on

1. Cardinal Worthing was scheduled to _____ the new bishop on the first day of the new year.

2. All the members of the nature club support the _____ that natural habitats for wild animals must be maintained.

3. The teachers decided not to _____ the students with homework during their spring vacation.

4. The doctor told Fred to say in bed, read a good book, and _____ large quantities of fruit juices.

5. Margaret, who wanted a big family, hoped to _____ her first child soon.

6. The students put forth the _____ that tennis and soccer be added to the school sports program.

7. Katherine liked her little brother, but taking care of him after school every day felt like a

_____ .

8. A ceremony was planned to _____ the new chapel.

9. Jonas loved to _____ complicated plots for science fiction stories, but he was not very good at getting them down on paper.

10. Eleanor went to concerts partly for the music and partly to _____ the excitement and high spirits generated by a live performance.

5:2 Roots Review
The incomplete sentences below contain words that you learned in the two roots lessons in this unit. Complete each sentence so that it makes sense and shows the meaning of the boldfaced vocabulary word.

1. Gregory felt that his **opponent** _____

_____ .

2. After Mr. Owens spoke, the **proponents** of his plan _____

_____ .

3. Max jokingly said that Ed was welcome at the party if he would **provide** _____

_____ .

4. "Jimmy," said Mrs. Carter, "You **provoke** me when you _____

_____ ."

5. The guide said that **provisions** for the climb to the mountain peak _____

_____ .

6. To **protest** the administration's attitude toward athletics, the students _____

_____ .

7. In her **hypercritical** way, Tania said " _____

_____ ."

8. Marcella is one of the most **provident** people I know. On the night of the blizzard, when the power went out, she _____

_____ .

9. Everyone in the class cheered when the teacher **proclaimed** _____

_____ .

10. Using **hyperbole**, which is typical for him, Henry said, " _____

_____ ."

5:3 Choosing Just the Right Word

Many of the words you have worked with in this unit have a number of synonyms. In some cases the synonyms have slightly different meanings.

Below are synonym studies for three of your vocabulary words, each followed by several incomplete sentences. Use either the vocabulary words or their synonyms to complete the sentences. Refer to the synonym studies as you decide which word carries the best meaning for each sentence.

solitude   isolation   seclusion

Solitude, isolation and *seclusion* all mean the state of being alone. *Solitude* implies either being apart from all people or choosing to be apart from the people one is usually near. *She enjoyed her few moments of solitude after work before the children got home.* Isolation stresses separation from others—often forced separation. *He was kept in isolation until the nature of the disease could be determined.* Seclusion suggests being shut away from others by choice. *They spent two weeks every summer in total seclusion in their cabin in the woods.*

1. Living with two roommates and a dormitory full of students limited Paula's opportunities for

_____ .

2. The Montgomerys enjoyed the _____ of their hideaway house in the

country.

3. After three days of _____ in a separate ward, the prisoner was

pleased to join the others in the mess hall.

resolve   decide

Resolve and *decide* both mean to come to a conclusion. *Resolve* implies a clear intention to do something. *She resolved to start her diet on January 2. Decide* implies the making of a decision or a judgment. *He finally decided on chocolate rather than strawberry.*

4. It took Marilyn four weeks to _____ on a color and style for the

dress she was having made for her brother's wedding.

5. "I _____ to study harder this term!" proclaimed Rose.

conceive   imagine   think

Conceive, imagine and *think* all mean to form an idea. *Conceive* suggests forming and developing an idea or plan. *He was able to conceive a plot for the play in only one week. Imagine* stresses picturing something in one's mind—visualizing. *Sue tried to imagine what Peru looks like. Think* implies having an idea in mind and working with the idea, but not the making of a decision or plan. *He didn't stop to think about the consequences.*

6. Thomas decided to take the time to sit and _____ about all the

things he and Mr. Macintosh had talked about.

7. Laurie's assignment was to _____ a design for the new toddler playground.

8. Denise likes to _____ herself as a member of a crew in a round-the-world sailboat race.

5:4 Recognizing Other Word Forms

Below are other forms of five of the vocabulary words for this unit. The story that follows contains five blanks. Fill in each blank with the correct word. Use what you have learned in this unit to help you figure out what the words mean.

conception   proposal   resolute   congeniality   solitary

Have you ever wondered how new products make their way to store shelves? It's a long process with many stages, starting with the _____ of an idea and its
_____ to a management committee. Next comes design, then production, and finally sales. In the initial stages, the job is largely a _____
one, requiring long hours of individual thought and planning. After the product is manufactured, the nature of the work changes. The important job of selling calls for an outgoing person.
_____ and a good sense of humor can help the salesperson as much as knowledge of the product itself. A good salesperson must also be persistent and
_____ in his determination to sell. Once on the shelf, the product requires good marketing, both inside the store and in the public media, to make it desirable and, with any luck, popular.

5:5 *Putting Your Vocabulary to Use*

The scrambled words below are all vocabulary words from this unit or the last one. Use the definition or synonym next to each scramble to help you figure out what the word is. Then write the word in the space provided. The number of lines in each answer space also provides a clue to the word. The circled letters will form the names of the authors of the two reading passages in this unit.

1. NACELIOGN — agreeable — _ _ _ _ _ _ _ _ Ⓞ

2. BEIBIM — drink — Ⓞ _ _ _ _ _

3. TERPOPNON — advocate — _ _ _ _ _ Ⓞ _ _ _

4. IDEBAATC — renounce — _ _ _ _ Ⓞ _ _ _

5. MELSHOWEO — healthful — _ _ Ⓞ _ _ _ _ _ _

6. EELSORV — determine — _ _ _ _ Ⓞ _ _

7. SONPIOPTOIR — statement — _ _ _ _ _ _ _ _ _ _ Ⓞ

8. VEKPORO — stir up — _ _ _ _ _ _ _

9. TERCADT — take away from — _ _ _ _ _ _ _

10. ROSTYLAI — alone — _ _ _ _ Ⓞ _ _ _

11. RELBEPHYO — exaggeration — Ⓞ _ _ _ _ _ _ _ _

12. CORDENVIPE — guidance — _ _ Ⓞ _ _ _ _ _ _ _

13. RWYA — cautious — _ _ Ⓞ _

14. IONCEECV — think up — _ _ _ _ _ _ Ⓞ _

15. TNOECCRESA — dedicate — _ _ _ _ _ _ _ Ⓞ _ _

16. CBAUDT — carry off by force — _ _ _ Ⓞ _ _

Names: _____

1: Meeting Words in Context

Reading Selection   Fresco Painting

Words Introduced   suited   previously   resume   results   revived

2: The Roots of Our Language

Roots Introduced   mega-   -polis   metro-   magni-   -fy
animus   -loqui   -tude

3: Meeting Words in Context

Reading Selection   Oil Painting

Words Introduced   fluid   reproduce   range   variation   intends

4: The Roots of Our Language

Roots Introduced   auto-   mobile   graph   -nym   pseudo-

5: Extending Your Word Power

Multiple Meanings
Roots Review
Using Words Precisely
Recognizing Other Word Forms
Putting Your Vocabulary to Use

1: Meeting Words in Context

Fresco Painting

Fresco painting is a technique in which the artist paints on a plastered wall while the plaster is still damp. Fresco artists decorate both inside and outside walls. Fresco painting is especially well **suited** to decorating large walls in churches, government buildings, and palaces.

A wall must be carefully plastered before an artist paints a fresco on it. Usually, several layers of plaster are applied. The first layers are somewhat coarse. The final layer, called the *intonaco,* is smooth and bright white. The artist may plaster the wall himself, but most artists employ plasterers to do this work. The artist or plasterer does not apply the intonaco over the entire wall at once. Instead, he applies just enough intonaco for one day's painting.

A fresco painter applies paint onto the wall while the plaster is still damp. The painter uses colors made of dry pigment that is mixed, in most cases, only with water. The plaster dries and hardens in about eight hours. The drying and hardening process seals the colors onto the wall.

The artist stops painting when the plaster is almost dry because the pigments—mixed only with water—will not stick to dry plaster. At the next working session, the artist gives the final coat of plaster to the area next to the part of the fresco that was finished **previously**. The artist then **resumes** painting, keeping the seam, or *join,* between the two sections as neat as possible.

Fresco plaster bleaches many colors. Therefore, not all pigments used in other painting techniques can be used in fresco painting. Fresco painters get the best **results** from soft, not too brilliant colors. These artists frequently use grays, rust tones, and tans.

Fresco painting reached its greatest popularity from the 1200's through the 1500's. Italy was the center of fresco painting during that period. During the 1900's, Mexican artists **revived** fresco painting. Mexican artists decorated many public buildings with large frescoes that show scenes from Mexican history.

Excerpted from *The World Book Encyclopedia.* © 1985 World Book, Inc.

Choose from the story two words that are unfamiliar to you or whose meanings you are not completely sure of. (Do not choose words that appear in boldfaced type.) Write the words on the lines provided below. Then, beside each word, write what you think it means, based on how it was used in the story.

1. _____ : _____

_____

2. _____ : _____

_____

When you have finished the exercises in this lesson, go to your dictionary and find the definitions for the words you entered above. If a word has more than one meaning, look for the one that defines the word as it is used in the story. Then write the words and their dictionary definitions in the Student Words pages at the back of the book. How close did you come to figuring out their meanings for yourself?

1:1 Using Context

Put an *x* in the box beside each correct answer. For clues to the meanings of the words, reread the parts of the passage in which they appear.

1. The fact that fresco painting is **suited** to decorating large walls means that the method
   - ☐ a. can only be used on large walls.
   - ☐ b. was invented for decorating large walls.
   - ☐ c. is appropriate for large surfaces.
   - ☐ d. is inappropriate for large surfaces.

2. The part that was finished **previously** was completed
   - ☐ a. earlier.
   - ☐ b. very quickly.
   - ☐ c. professionally.
   - ☐ d. later.

3. To **resume** painting means to
   - ☐ a. enjoy it.
   - ☐ b. forget about it.
   - ☐ c. finish it.
   - ☐ d. begin again after an interruption.

4. To get the best **results** from certain colors means to
   - ☐ a. enjoy using them the most.
   - ☐ b. get the best effects from them.
   - ☐ c. get the most for your money.
   - ☐ d. get the best adhesion from them.

5. The Mexican artists who **revived** fresco painting
   - ☐ a. disliked the method.
   - ☐ b. discovered old fresco paintings.
   - ☐ c. argued against its usefulness.
   - ☐ d. brought it into use again.

1:2 Making Connections

In this exercise, the list of vocabulary words is followed by definitions of the words as they are used in the story. Write each word in front of its definition.

suited   previously   resume   result   revive

1. _____ : outcome; good or useful effect

2. _____ : appropriate or fitting

3. _____ : bring back into use or fashion

4. _____ : begin again; go on from where one left off

5. _____ : before; earlier

1:3 Making Connections

Write each vocabulary word on the line in front of the appropriate synonym and antonym.

suited   previously   resume   result   revive

	synonym	antonym
1. _____	before	after
2. _____	renew	end
3. _____	restart	quit
4. _____	effect	cause
5. _____	fitted	mismatched

1:4 Making Connections

Complete each sentence with the correct vocabulary word.

suited   previously   resume   results   revive

1. School is scheduled to _____ on January 3, after a two-week vacation.

2. Orchids, which grow in the tropics, are not _____ to the cold climate of the north.

3. The twins' decision to stop wearing the same clothes brought the desired _____ . People could finally tell them apart.

4. Elaine hoped to _____ her sister's interest in dance by taking her to the ballet.

5. Because she had visited the museum _____ , Kathy was able to lead her cousin to the most interesting exhibits.

2: The Roots of Our Language

mega- The prefix *mega-* means large. A megalopolis (meg-uh-LOP-uh-lus) is an extremely large city or a region that embraces many large cities with no rural stretches between them. New York City is a megalopolis in the first sense. The region between Washington, D.C., and Boston, Massachusetts, given its current growth rate, will be the second type of megalopolis in the near future.

-polis The root *-polis*, which you see in *megalopolis*, comes from Greek and means city. We also see *-polis* in *metropolis*, which is a major city. One of the

metro- meanings of *metro-* is womb, which is the female body part in which unborn babies are nurtured. Hence, *metropolis* means mother city.

Mega- can also mean one million. A *megavolt* is one million volts, and a *megameter* is one million meters.

You may have heard the expression "delusions of grandeur." We trust you have not heard it applied to you. Anyway, another word for this condition is *megalomania* (MEG-uh-lo-MAY-nee-uh). A person suffering from this condition has an exaggerated sense of self-love and thinks, incorrectly, that he or she is great, famous, wealthy or various combinations thereof. Such a person is called a *megalomaniac* (MEG-uh-lo-MAY-nee-ak). *Maniac* comes from a Greek word meaning to be insane, so *megalomania* means literally to be insane about the imagined large place one occupies in the world.

magni- Another prefix that means large or great is the Latin *magni-*. If you

-fy combine *magni-* with the suffix *-fy*, which means to make or to cause to be, you get *magnify*, which means to make greater. No doubt at one time or another you have looked through a *magnifying* glass to make something appear bigger—very fine print that is hard to read, for example. *Magnitude* is

-tude made up of the prefix *magni-* and the suffix *-tude*, which means the state or quality of. *Magnitude* has more than one meaning. It can mean large as in the sentence *The sheer magnitude of this job overwhelms me.* It can also mean simply size, not necessarily large size: *This job is of a small magnitude; we'll do it in a day.* Or it can mean the quality or importance of something: *The Supreme Court decision was of such magnitude it has altered the course of United States history.*

At some time in your life you may have been a little hurt or offended and had someone tell you to "be big about it." They might also have told you to be *magnanimous* (mag-NAN-uh-mus). Of course you know by now that the prefix on that word means large or great. The rest of the word comes from

animus the root *animus*, which means spirit. Thus, *magnanimous* means showing a great or lofty spirit. Those who possess such a spirit are generous in their opinions of other people, even when those other people do them harm. In other words, if a magnanimous person is offended, he or she is going to "be big about it."

-loqui When you combine *magni-* with *-loqui*, a root meaning to speak, you arrive at *magniloquent* (mag-NIL-uh-kwunt). It describes someone who is fond of using large words. The *-loqui* root appears again in *loquacious* (lo-KWAY-shus), which also has to do with talking—talking a lot, in fact, for that's what it means. On the other hand, *eloquent* (EL-uh-kwunt) people speak expressively and with clear meaning. Such people do not use too many big words just for the sake of using big words. Such people do not talk too much. And finally, such people know when to stop talking.

2:1   Write each word or root listed on the left beside its meaning on the right.

-loqui   1. _____ generous

-polis   2. _____ size

mega-   3. _____ city

magnitude   4. _____ large

magnanimous   5. _____ speech

2:2   Mark each statement as either true or false.

_____   1. A megalomaniac is a person with exaggerated ideas about his or her own importance.

_____   2. A loquacious person is a good conversationalist.

_____   3. A magniloquent speaker speaks simply and clearly.

_____   4. An eloquent speaker usually will attract an audience.

_____   5. An urban region containing several large cities is a metropolis.

2:3   Answer the following questions.

1. If *magnitude* refers to largeness, what would exactitude refer to? _____

_____

2. Would a megalomaniac usually be known for his humbleness? _____

_____

3. How would you describe the magnitude of a mouse? _____

4. If you magnify your friends' faults, will they be pleased? _____

_____

5. When the mayor of a small town refers to the town as "a growing metropolis," is he exaggerating or being humble? _____

3: Meeting Words in Context

Oil Painting

Oil paint is made by mixing powdered pigments with a binder of vegetable oil. Linseed oil is the most common binder. Artists buy oil paints in the form of thick pastes packaged in tubes. If an artist wants his paint to be more **fluid**, he adds a painting medium made of linseed oil, varnish, and turpentine.

Certain features of oil paint make it popular with artists who want to show the natural appearance of the world around them. Oil paint dries slowly. Therefore, the artist has time to blend his strokes into each other carefully and to adjust his color mixtures to **reproduce** natural appearances. Oil paint—even when applied thickly—does not crack so easily as does water paint or egg tempera. As a result, the artist can apply oil paint in varying thicknesses to produce a wide **range** of textures.

Each artist develops his own method of working with oil paint. Many use some **variation** of the following steps. First, the artist puts on his wooden palette a small dab of each color he **intends** to use. The artist can mix colors on the palette to produce new tones. A small cup clipped to the corner of the palette holds paint thinner.

Usually, before he starts painting, he draws the important outlines on his canvas or panel with charcoal or a pencil. Some artists attempt to achieve their final effects immediately. They paint all the colors and details in a few sessions or even at a single session. This method is called *direct painting* or *alla prima*. If an artist can use this method without making any corrections, his picture will appear lively, natural, and unified.

Excerpted from *The World Book Encyclopedia*. © 1985 World Book, Inc.

Choose from the story two words that are unfamiliar to you or whose meanings you are not completely sure of. (Do not choose words that appear in boldfaced type.) Write the words on the lines provided below. Then, beside each word, write what you think it means, based on how it was used in the story.

1. _____ : _____

_____

2. _____ : _____

_____

When you have finished the exercises in this lesson, go to your dictionary and find the definitions for the words you entered above. If a word has more than one meaning, look for the one that defines the word as it is used in the story. Then write the words and their dictionary definitions in the Student Words pages at the back of the book. How close did you come to figuring out their meanings for yourself?

3:1 Using Context

Below are five sentences from the reading passage. From the four answer choices that follow each sentence, choose the one that gives the best definition of the boldfaced word in the sentence. Put an *x* in the box beside it. Use the context, or setting, provided by the sentence to help you discover the meaning of the word. If the sentence itself does not provide enough clues to the word, go back to the passage and read the paragraph in which the sentence appears.

1. If an artist wants his paint to be more **fluid**, he adds a painting medium made of linseed oil, varnish, and turpentine.
   - ☐ a. thick
   - ☐ b. liquid
   - ☐ c. brightly colored
   - ☐ d. easy to remove

2. Therefore, the artist has time to blend his strokes into each other carefully and to adjust his color mixtures to **reproduce** natural appearances.
   - ☐ a. contrast with
   - ☐ b. give birth to
   - ☐ c. make exactly like
   - ☐ d. eliminate

3. As a result, the artist can apply oil paint in varying thicknesses to produce a wide **range** of textures.
   - ☐ a. variety
   - ☐ b. roughness
   - ☐ c. strip
   - ☐ d. palette

4. Many use some **variation** of the following steps.
   - ☐ a. hint or clue
   - ☐ b. color
   - ☐ c. slightly changed form
   - ☐ d. number

5. First, the artist puts on his wooden palette a small dab of each color he **intends** to use
   - ☐ a. dislikes
   - ☐ b. plans
   - ☐ c. hopes
   - ☐ d. asks

3:2 Making Connections

Listed below are the five vocabulary words from the reading passage, followed by ten words or phrases that are related to them in some way. The ten words or phrases may be synonyms, antonyms or definitions. On the line next to each word or phrase, write the vocabulary word that is related to it.

fluid   reproduce   range   variation   intend

1. sameness _____

2. mean _____

3. copy exactly _____

4. solid _____

5. difference _____

6. flowing _____

7. spectrum _____

8. imitate _____

9. have as a purpose _____

10. a series between limits _____

3:3 Making Connections

Complete the following analogies by inserting one of the five vocabulary words in the blank at the end of each one. Remember that in an analogy the last two words or phrases must be related to each other in the same way that the first two are related.

fluid   reproduce   variation   range   intend

1. ask : request : : plan : _____

2. excitement : calm : : sameness : _____

3. full : inflate : : same : _____

4. rock : solid : : water : _____

5. hint : clue : : choice : _____

3:4 Making Connections

Complete each sentence with the correct vocabulary word.

fluid   reproduce   range   variation   intend

1. Roberta added bananas to the chocolate cake she was baking, as a _____ on her mother's usual recipe.

2. The Scanlons had dozens of photographs from their trip to New York, but the camera could not _____ the feeling of the trip.

3. On roller skates, Victor's movements were _____ and graceful.

4. Mr. Phelps did not _____ to prevent his students from continuing their discussion of the way in which grades are determined.

5. Miguel felt overwhelmed by the _____ of different bicycles he had to choose from.

4: The Roots of Our Language

auto-

You have seen the prefix *auto-* many times, and you've probably ridden many times in a vehicle that uses the prefix as part of its name—the automobile. An automobile, of course, is a self-powered machine that moves. *Auto-* means

mobile

self. *Mobile* means capable of moving. That accounts for the name of what may be the most popular vehicle in history.

Now that you know that *auto-* means self, you can decode a good many words. For example, in Unit 7 you learned about the suffix *-crat,* which means rule, especially governmental rule. If a democrat is a person who believes in and participates in the rule of the people, what do you think an autocrat is? Sure enough, an autocrat is a ruler who answers only to himself. He makes all the rules and enforces them with complete authority. Another familiar word is *autograph.* We usually think of an autograph as being a famous person's signature. Famous people are often asked to give their auto-

graph

graphs to fans. But let's look at the roots. *Graph* means to write. We see it in *photograph* (FOH-tuh-graf), which means literally writing with light, and *phonograph* (FOH-nuh-graf), which means writing with sound. So, if you think about *auto-* combined with *-graph,* you realize that every time you write your signature you are signing your autograph.

-nym

Here is one you may not know: *autonym* (AW-tuh-nim). The suffix *-nym* means name, so an autonym is your real name. My real name, you might ask, as opposed to my imaginary name? Well, yes, in a way. Some people, namely movie stars, writers and people on the wrong side of the law, use false names, or pseudonyms (SOOD-un-ims). The prefix *pseudo-* means false.

pseudo-

So if you get a movie star's autograph, you might get an autonym, or you might get a pseudonym. It all depends on whether Christopher J. Throb was actually born Ferdinand Glummelshwatz or not.

Most of us are familiar with the word *autopsy* (AW-top-see). We understand it as being the examination of a dead body to determine the cause of death. But that is only one of the meanings of autopsy; it actually has a broader definition. The *op* part of the word comes from a Greek word meaning sight. Thus, the general meaning of *autopsy* is to see with one's own eyes. As a result, it can be applied to any critical examination of a thing from the past, be it an event, a work of art or literature, or a personality.

You will have no trouble figuring out that *autosuggestion* (AW-toh-sug-JES-chun) means self-suggestion. But what exactly is self-suggestion? It's a technique that involves giving yourself positive thoughts so that you can influence your behavior for the good. A French psychologist named Emile Coue told his patients to repeat this suggestion often: "Every day, in every way, I am getting better and better." Patients who repeated that auto-suggestion faithfully, Coue believed, actually would get better and better. You might use the technique yourself, to try to break a bad habit or to create a good one. But, as you have learned from this lesson, you must concern your-self with your *self,* and with things you can control. How about this: "Every day, in every way, my work on my vocabulary will get better and better." It can't hurt.

4:1 Write each word or root listed on the left beside its meaning on the right.

pseudonym   1. _____ self

mobile   2. _____ absolute ruler

auto-   3. _____ able to move

autocrat   4. _____ name

-nym   5. _____ false name

4:2 Mark each statement as either true or false.

_____ 1. An autocrat believes that people should have the power to rule themselves.

_____ 2. One way to get rid of a bad habit might be through autosuggestion.

_____ 3. One way to hide your real identity as a writer is to use an autonym.

_____ 4. The root meaning of *photograph* is "sound writing."

_____ 5. Autograph collectors collect signatures of famous people.

4:3 Put an *x* in the box beside each answer you think is correct.

1. Something that is pseudoscientific is

☐ a. not really scientific.   ☐ b. proved through experiment.   ☐ c. highly scientific.

2. Someone who assumes complete authority is

☐ a. a bureaucrat.   ☐ b. a democrat.   ☐ c. an autocrat.

3. Something that moves under its own power is

☐ a. motive.   ☐ b. missive.   ☐ c. mobile.

4. In seeking a cause of death, doctors often perform an

☐ a. autopsy.   ☐ b. biopsy.   ☐ c. autonomy.

5. A false name is called

☐ a. an autocrat.   ☐ b. an autonym.   ☐ c. a pseudonym.

5:Extending Your Word Power

5:1 Multiple Meanings
Below are four vocabulary words you met in this unit. Each has more than one meaning. Use the words to fill in the blanks in the sentences that follow. In some of the sentences, the word has a meaning that is different from the meaning it has in the passage you read. If you are unsure of the various meanings of a word, look the word up in the glossary.

suit   revive   reproduce   range

1. Rescue workers were able to _____ the elderly man who had passed out from the heat.

2. Rabbits are known to _____ in extremely large numbers.

3. Gordon discovered that stamp collecting was the perfect hobby to _____ his unathletic nature.

4. Some New York designers tried hard to _____ the miniskirt fashion of the sixties.

5. The eight Warner children _____ in age from five to seventeen.

6. The _____ brought against Mr. Rizzo's company for hiring illegal immigrants was bad for business.

7. Rebecca had taught herself to _____ the calls of a number of kinds of birds.

8. When babies are first born their _____ of vision is very limited.

5:2 Roots Review

The incomplete sentences below contain words that you learned in the two roots lessons in this unit. Complete each sentence so that it makes sense and shows the meaning of the boldfaced vocabulary word.

1. Driving down the highway, Don knew that he was in a **megalopolis** by the fact that _____ _____ .

2. It was clear that Gladys was suffering from **megalomania** from the way she _____ _____ .

3. No one had guessed the **magnitude** of Wendell's wealth until the safe was opened and it was discovered that _____ _____ .

4. Growing **loquacious**, the traveler _____ _____ .

5. Mr. Theodore became known as the **autocrat** of the hair salon after _____ _____ .

6. Surprising his workers with his **magnanimous** act, the owner of the company _____ _____ .

7. Betsy Sue Plunkett used a **pseudonym** for _____ _____ .

8. The **mobile** military unit could _____ _____ .

9. All those present at the **autopsy** confessed that they had never _____ _____ .

10. Lydia's plea for mercy was so **eloquent** that _____ _____ .

5:3 Choosing Just the Right Word

Many of the words you have worked with in this unit have a number of synonyms. In some cases the synonyms are slightly different in meaning. When you write and speak, it is up to you to choose the words that express your ideas as strongly and clearly as possible.

In this exercise, synonym studies are provided for three of your vocabulary words. Use either the vocabulary words or their synonyms to complete the sentences in the exercise. Refer to the synonym studies as you decide which word carries the best meaning for the specific context of each sentence.

imitate   reproduce

> *Imitate* and *reproduce* both have to do with copying. To imitate is to try to copy someone's action, sound or style. *Jack liked to imitate his father's walk.* To reproduce is to make an identical copy of a thing. *The artist could not reproduce the colors of the leaves exactly.*

1. Clair tried to _____ in her own yard the lovely flower garden she

   had seen at her uncle's house.

2. When learning to speak, babies _____ the sounds they hear from the

   people around them.

revive   refresh

> The words *revive* and *refresh* both concern bringing a person or thing back to a lively state. To revive is to bring back to life something that has fallen into disuse or ill health over time. *The play was revived twenty years after its original production.* To refresh is to bring new vibrancy, energy or strength to something that has faded or weakened. *Nancy planned to refresh her room with a new coat of paint.*

3. There was an attempt on the part of some of the townspeople to

   _____ the tradition of an annual community picnic.

4. Having driven two hundred miles without a stop, Jim and Henry decided to

   _____ themselves with a hearty lunch.

plan   intend

> *Plan* and *intend* are verbs that describe different kinds of thinking about an action before the action is taken. To plan is to decide beforehand how something is to be done. *The entire family helped plan the trip to Washington.* To intend means to have a particular purpose in mind. *Claire intended to save all her money for new clothes.*

5. Leah did not _____ to have anything to do with her sister's scheme to skip school on Friday.

6. The drama club scheduled a meeting for anyone interested in helping to

_____ the next production.

5:4 Recognizing Other Word Forms

Listed below are seven of the vocabulary words from this unit, along with several different forms of each word. The story that follows contains seven blanks. Fill in each blank with some form of one of the words listed below. You will use one form of each vocabulary word.

intends   intention   intended   intending   **suited**   suit   suitable

variation   various   variety   vary   **results**   result   resulted   resulting

fluid   fluidity   **range**   ranged   ranging

revived   reviving   revival

Joe was not in a good mood. He stood in the garage staring at the

_____ draining from the '84 Corvette he was working on. He thought
       1

about a hundred things, _____ from fast cars to elegant dates with his
          2

girlfriend to a trip to California. All of them had one thing in common: they required lots of

money. Joe _____ to earn that money somehow.
     3

Unfortunately, the only job really _____ for him was simple car
         4

maintenance. "Nothing wrong with being a grease monkey," he thought, "but it won't

_____ in the really big bucks I want." The paycheck Joe received for
   5

forty hours of pumping gas and changing oil was not large. At the end of every month, he was

just about broke. And that sad condition always brought about a _____
          6

of his desire for ready cash. Joe yearned for the day when he could begin to taste the

_____ of experiences that for now he could only dream of.
   7

5:5 Putting Your Vocabulary to Use

Use vocabulary words from this unit and the last unit to complete
the crossword puzzle.

ACROSS

3. overly active
7. official announcement
8. bring back
9. begin again after an interval
11. slight change
13. space of more than three dimensions
14. large urban area including several cities

DOWN

1. careful in preparing for the future
2. large city
4. heavy weight
5. vividly expressive
6. fake name
9. bring new energy
10. coming before or earlier
12. size

Going Haywire

Have you ever wondered where the expression "going haywire" came from? Well, the origin of the phrase is actually tangled up with hay and wire. In 1828, a man named Moses Bliss invented a press for making hay bales. Farmers had previously used simple wooden boxes to shape hay into bales, and they had laboriously tied the hay together by hand with string. Bliss's invention consisted of a power press that packed the hay into tight, firm bundles, and a mechanism that wrapped the bundles with wire. Quite a time and energy saver. The only problem with the early hay presses was that the stiff wire often went out of control and became tangled around horses, farmers and the machines themselves. In the hay fields, such mishaps were known as "going haywire," and the expression was soon being applied to plans that went astray or to situations that got out of control.

Student Words

Word	Definition

Word

Definition

Word

Definition

Word

Definition

Word

Definition

Word   **Definition**

Word   **Definition**

Word

Definition

Word

Definition

Word   **Definition**

_____   _____

_____   _____

_____   _____

_____   _____

_____   _____

_____   _____

_____   _____

_____   _____

_____   _____

_____   _____

_____   _____

_____   _____

_____   _____

_____   _____

_____   _____

_____   _____

_____   _____

_____   _____

_____   _____

_____   _____

_____   _____

_____   _____

Word   **Definition**

UNIT ONE

1:1

1. c   2. d   3. a   4. d   5. a

1:2

1. group / individual
2. gain / lose
3. substitute / competitor
4. closed / opened
5. experienced / untried

1:3

1. understudy   2. folded   3. attain   4. seasoned   5. troupe

1:4

1. attain   2. seasoned   3. troupe   4. folded   5. understudy

2:1

1. prejudice   2. pre-   3. precede   4. con-   5. diction

2:2

1. false   2. true   3. true   4. false   5. false

2:3

1. when you send in the order
2. prejudice
3. The person speaks aloud and records what he or she says.
4. to come together in a crowd
5. predicts

3:1

1. d   2. b   3. a   4. c   5. b

3:2

1. tribulations   2. graduated   3. cult   4. decade   5. distinctive

3:3

1. graduated   2. tribulations   3. distinctive   4. tribulations   5. cult

6. decade   7. tribulations   8. graduated   9. cult   10. distinctive

3:4

1. graduated   2. tribulations   3. distinctive   4. cult   5. decade

4:1

1. bi-   2. forte   3. bicentennial   4. complete   5. compose

4:2

1. true	2. false	3. true	4. true	5. false

4:3

1. one that requires both hands
2. compose
3. an animal with two feet
4. complete
5. the binary system

5:1

1. a	2. c	3. b	4. b	5. c
6. a	7. a			

5:2

Answers will vary.

5:3

1. acquired	2. attain	3. acquired	4. attain	5. distinctive
6. peculiar	7. peculiar	8. distinctive		

5:4

1. distinction	2. attainment	3. attainable	4. folding	5. graduation

5:5

1. compose	2. tribulation	3. decode	4. precede	5. understudy
6. diction	7. combine	8. acquire	9. precook	10. prehistoric
11. troupe	12. complete	13. seasoned	14. peculiar	

UNIT TWO

1:1

1. b	2. a	3. d	4. c	5. a

1:2

1. indicate	2. submissive	3. direct	4. posture	5. submissive
6. originate	7. direct	8. direct	9. indicate	10. originate
11. submissive	12. posture	13. indicate	14. submissive	

1:3

1. indicate	2. submissive	3. direct	4. originate	5. posture

1:4

1. posture 2. direct 3. submissive 4. indicate 5. originated

2:1

1. adopt 2. adhere 3. apt 4. adjacent 5. minister

2:2

1. true 2. false 3. false 4. false 5. false

2:3

1. a 2. c 3. a 4. c 5. b

3:1

1. b 2. a 3. d 4. a 5. b

3:2

1. eliminate 2. remedy 3. discipline 4. reduce 5. confine

3:3

1. disciplined 2. eliminate 3. reduce 4. confined 5. remedy

3:4

1. confined 2. remedy 3. disciplined 4. reduce 5. eliminate

4:1

1. dis- 2. lodge 3. orient 4. -logy 5. discontinue

4:2

1. false 2. false 3. true 4. false 5. false

4:3

1. They've knocked it down.
2. your identity or appearance
3. disoriented
4. disease
5. the study of the earth

5:1

1. reduced 2. originated 3. posture 4. reduced 5. disciplined

5:2

Answers will vary.

5:3

1. limits 2. confine 3. confined 4. submissive 5. obedient

6. began 7. originated 8. originated

5:4

1. discipline   2. submit   3. remedied   4. origin   5. confines

6. reduction   7. indication

5:5

UNIT THREE

1:1

1. stopping   ending   closing
2. give   apply
3. did   carried out
4. serious   unfriendly
5. energetic   happy

1:2

1. conducted   2. discontinue   3. stern   4. sprightly   5. devote

1:3

1. discontinue   2. stern   3. sprightly   4. conduct   5. devote

1:4

1. conducted   2. sprightly   3. devote   4. stern   5. discontinuing

2:1

| 1. immobile | 2. incapable | 3. illegible | 4. in- | 5. nonsense |

2:2

| 1. false | 2. true | 3. true | 4. false | 5. false |

2:3

| 1. c | 2. b | 3. a | 4. c | 5. c |

3:1

| 1. b | 2. c | 3. a | 4. c | 5. a |

3:2

1. shrewd	2. fulfilled	3. exceeded	4. sustained	5. formally
6 sustained	7. exceeded	8. shrewd	9. formally	10. exceeded
11. fulfilled	12. sustained	13. shrewd	14. formally	

3:3

| 1. shrewd | 2. exceeded | 3. sustained | 4. fulfilled | 5. formally |

3:4

| 1. formally | 2. exceeded | 3. fulfilled | 4. sustained | 5. shrewd |

4:1

| 1. exclude | 2. ex- | 3. cava | 4. exclusive | 5. expire |

4:2

| 1. false | 2. false | 3. false | 4. true | 5. true |

4:3

| 1. exhale | 2. excavated | 3. exclusive | 4. expired | 5. exterior |

5:1

| 1. sustain | 2. conducted | 3. formally | 4. devote | 5. fulfilled |

5:2

Answers will vary.

5:3

| 1. discontinue | 2. pause | 3. shrewd | 4. clever | 5. intelligent |

5:4

| 1. excess | 2. sustenance | 3. formalized | 4. fulfillment | 5. conductor |
| 6. devotion | | | | |

5:5

1. remedy 2. discontinue 3. illegal 4. confined 5. uncivilized

6. posture 7. stern 8. devotion 9. exclude 10. disguise

11. nonprofit 12. sprightly 13. adjacent 14. excavate 15. conducted

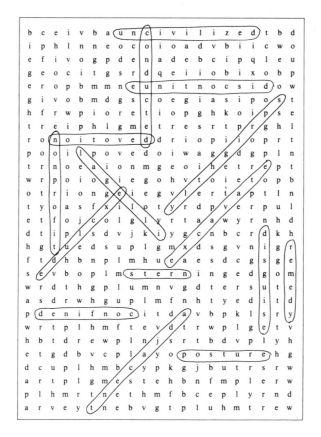

UNIT FOUR

1:1

1. b 2. c 3. a 4. b 5. d

1:2

1. mere 2. fixed 3. interlude 4. restored 5. effects

1:3

1. mere 2. fixed 3. restored 4. interlude 5. mere

6. effects 7. mere 8. interlude 9. interlude 10. mere

11. effects 12. fixed 13. fixed 14. restored

1:4

1. restored   2. fixed   3. mere   4. interlude   5. effects

2:1

1. decompose   2. deduce   3. duc   4. de-   5. detect

2:2

1. true   2. false   3. true   4. false   5. false

2:3

1. c   2. c   3. b   4. a   5. c

3:1

1. put into circulation
2. difficult
3. modest
4. plenty
5. accepted

3:2

1. distributed   kept
2. difficult   easy
3. modest   boastful
4. plentifulness   lack
5. assumed   rejected

3:3

1. humble   2. adopted   3. issued   4. trying   5. abundance

3:4

1. humble   2. abundance   3. issued   4. adopted   5. trying

4:1

1. ply   2. pro-   3. recede   4. inject   5. re-

4:2

1. false   2. true   3. false   4. false   5. true

4:3

1. c   2. a   3. b   4. a   5. b

5:1

1. a   2. b   3. c   4. b   5. a

6. b

5:2

Answers will vary.

5:3

1. restored
2. trying
3. repair
4. renew
5. difficult

5:4

1. restoration
2. humility
3. abundant
4. fixedly
5. adoption
6. merely

5:5

1. humble
2. decode
3. trying
4. effects
5. repay
6. abundance
7. replica
8. inhabited
9. improper
10. expire
11. recede
12. recess
13. fixed
14. deduct
15. issue
16. deduction
17. interlude

Phrase: log cabin president

UNIT FIVE

1:1

1. c
2. d
3. b
4. d
5. a

1:2

1. inborn   acquired
2. skilled   inept
3. effort   laziness
4. succeeding   losing
5. yielded   conquered

1:3

1. diligence
2. succumb
3. adept
4. prevail
5. innate

1:4

1. adept
2. prevailing
3. innate
4. succumbed
5. diligence

2:1

1. -fer
2. ex-
3. im-
4. port
5. trans-

2:2

1. true
2. true
3. false
4. false
5. true

2:3

1. a
2. b
3. b
4. c
5. c

3:1

1. a
2. d
3. c
4. a
5. b

3:2

1. affix
2. vigorous
3. incorporate
4. propel
5. delineate

3:3

| 1. propel | 2. delineate | 3. vigorous | 4. incorporating | 5. affixed |

3:4

| 1. propel | 2. delineating | 3. incorporate | 4. affixed | 5. vigorous |

4:1

| 1. invigorate | 2. interval | 3. interfere | 4. inter- | 5. -sect |

4:2

| 1. true | 2. true | 3. false | 4. false | 5. false |

4:3

1. You are cutting the frog apart.
2. In an interview, the talk takes place between two people.
3. interval
4. It gets in the way of the sound.
5. intercept

5:1

| 1. delineate | 2. prevail | 3. delineate | 4. incorporate | 5. prevail |
| 6. incorporate | 7. prevail | 8. delineate | 9. incorporate | 10. prevail |

5:2

Answers will vary.

5:3

| 1. strenuous | 2. vigorous | 3. strenuous | 4. attach | 5. attach |
| 6. affix | 7. push | 8. propel | 9. propel | |

5:4

| 1. innately | 2. affixing | 3. vigor | 4. prevailed | 5. diligently |
| 6. propeller | 7. incorporation | 8. delineation | 9. invigorating | 10. propulsion |

5:5

1. innate	2. humility	3. succumb	4. transport	5. reject
6. prevail	7. prefer	8. mere	9. vigor	10. infer
11. strenuous	12. affix	13. propel	14. transfer	15. detect
16. restored				

Phrase: <u>hole in one</u>

UNIT SIX

1:1

| 1. c | 2. a | 3. d | 4. a | 5. b |

1:2

1. agile	2. credit	3. interval	4. offset	5. offset
6. interval	7. versatile	8. agile	9. credit	10. versatile

1:3

1. agile	2. versatile	3. interval	4. offset	5. credit

1:4

1. versatile	2. offset	3. agile	4. interval	5. credit

2:1

1. subscribe	2. sub-	3. submerge	4. marine	5. scribe

2:2

1. false	2. false	3. false	4. false	5. true

2:3

1. b	2. a	3. c	4. a	5. c

3:1

1. d	2. c	3. a	4. c	5. a

3:2

1. inclined	2. execute	3. relatively	4. versed	5. ultimately

3:3

1. performing   undoing
2. finally   firstly
3. comparatively   completely
4. willing   uninterested
5. experienced   ignorant

3:4

1. inclined	2. executing	3. relatively	4. versed	5. ultimately

4:1

1. oversight	2. overwhelm	3. overstate	4. oversee	5. over-

4:2

1. false	2. true	3. false	4. false	5. true

4:3

1. overpopulation	2. overseer	3. overreacting	4. above your head	5. overwhelmed

5:1

1. offset	2. inclined	3. credit	4. execute	5. inclined
6. credit	7. offset			

5:2

Answers will vary.

5:3

1. pause   2. versed   3. interval   4. final   5. skilled

6. ultimate

5:4

1. versatility   offsetting
2. executed   agility
3. credited   ultimate
4. ultimatum   execution
5. inclination   relation

5:5

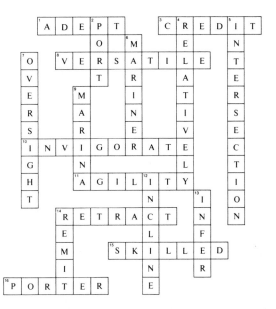

UNIT SEVEN

1:1

1. d   2. b   3. c   4. c   5. b

1:2

1. secure   2. removed   3. exerting   4. excelled   5. removed

6. excelled   7. anticipation   8. secure   9. exerting   10. anticipation

1:3

1. removed   2. excelled   3. secure   4. anticipation   5. exert

1:4

1. exerting   2. removed   3. excelled   4. secure   5. anticipation

2:1

1. misconception   2. misinterpretation   3. misconstrue   4. mis-   5. miscalculate

2:2

1. true   2. false   3. true   4. true   5. true

2:3

1. improper or bad behavior
2. to misunderstand
3. misplace
4. lost
5. misquote him

3:1

1. d   2. a   3. c   4. d   5. d

3:2

1. acquaintance   2. demure   3. snare   4. steal   5. rare

3:3

1. snared   2. demure   3. acquaintances   4. rare   5. steal

3:4

1. snared   2. demure   3. stole   4. rare   5. acquaintances

4:1

1. epidemic   2. epitaph   3. epigraph   4. epi-   5. epidermis

4:2

1. false   2. false   3. true   4. true   5. false

4:3

1. a   2. b   3. a   4. b   5. a

5:1

1. snare   2. removed   3. secure   4. stolen   5. rare

5:2

Answers will vary.

5:3

1. catch   2. rare   3. snare   4. excel   5. uncommon

6. catch   7. exceeds   8. rare   9. exceed

5:4

1. anticipatory   rarely
2. removal   excellent
3. demurely   steal
4. acquaint   security
5. exertion   snare

5:5

1. misconstrue   2. acquaint   3. anticipation   4. snare   5. rare

6. epitaph   7. demure   8. secure   9. submerge   10. scribe

11. excel   12. exert   13. demos   14. execute   15. overstate

16. ultimatum   17. epidermis

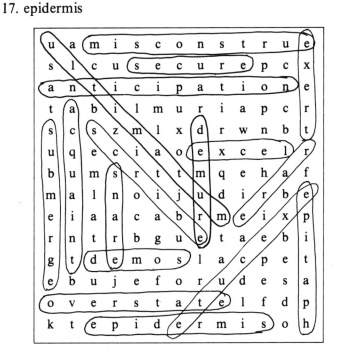

UNIT EIGHT

1:1

1. hold in check
2. on guard
3. last mentioned
4. cause to judge wrongly
5. showing no favoritism

1:2

1. control   increase
2. cautious   trusting
3. last   first
4. distort   clarify
5. unbiased   prejudiced

1:3

1. latter   2. impartial   3. wary   4. warp   5. curb

1:4

1. warp   2. curb   3. latter   4. impartial   5. wary

2:1

1. ob-   2. ligament   3. noxious   4. obligated   5. -ject

2:2

1. true   2. false   3. true   4. true   5. false

2:3

1. b   2. a   3. c   4. c   5. a

3:1

1. d   2. b   3. d   4. c   5. a

3:2

1. efficient   2. poses   3. strain   4. unique   5. procrastinate

3:3

1. strain   2. unique   3. procrastinate   4. efficient   5. pose

3:4

1. poses   2. procrastinate   3. efficient   4. strain   5. unique

4:1

1. abstain   2. solvent   3. dictator   4. dictate   5. duct

4:2

1. true   2. false   3. true   4. true   5. true

4:3

1. c   2. a   3. b   4. c   5. b

5:1

1. strain   2. curb   3. warp   4. strain   5. pose

6. warp

5:2

Answers will vary.

5:3

1. delay   2. efficient   3. wary   4. effective   5. procrastinate

6. cautious

5:4

1. efficiency   2. impartiality   3. posing   4. procrastination   5. uniqueness

6. wariness

5 : 5

1. efficient	2. warp	3. obliterate	4. curbs	5. interpret
6. abstain	7. duct	8. objective	9. pose	10. procrastinate
11. stole	12. noxious	13. strain	14. epigraph	15. misconstrue
16. ligament				

Phrase: <u>false advertising</u>

UNIT NINE

1 : 1

1. a	2. c	3. b	4. c	5. a

1 : 2

1. detract	2. conceived	3. resolve	4. proposition	5. consecrate

1 : 3

1. detract	2. conceive	3. consecrate	4. detract	5. resolve
6. proposition	7. consecrate	8. resolve	9. conceive	10. proposition

1 : 4

1. consecrated	2. resolve	3. proposition	4. detract	5. conceived

2 : 1

1. hyperbole	2. hypersonic	3. hypermnesia	4. hyper-	5. hyperactive

2 : 2

1. false	2. false	3. true	4. false	5. true

2 : 3

1. Because we don't know if it even exists—it is a kind of space we don't know about.
2. yes
3. remember things extremely well
4. Because he or she would find it difficult to stay in such a small space for so long.
5. hypersensitive

3 : 1

1. c	2. b	3. d	4. c	5. a

3 : 2

1. burden	2. solitude	3. wholesome	4. imbibe	5. congenial

3 : 3

1. absorb   emit
2. agreeable   unsuitable
3. load   help
4. beneficial   unhealthy
5. aloneness   companionship

3:4

1. congenial   2. solitude   3. imbibe   4. wholesome   5. burden

4:1

1. providence   2. pro-   3. provision   4. proponent   5. proclaim

4:2

1. false   2. true   3. true   4. false   5. true

4:3

1. a   2. c   3. b   4. b   5. a

5:1

1. consecrate   2. proposition   3. burden   4. imbibe   5. conceive

6. proposition   7. burden   8. consecrate   9. conceive   10. imbibe

5:2

Answers will vary.

5:3

1. solitude   2. seclusion   3. isolation   4. decide   5. resolve

6. think   7. conceive   8. imagine

5:4

1. conception   2. proposal   3. solitary   4. congeniality   5. resolute

5:5

1. congenial   2. imbibe   3. proponent   4. abdicate   5. wholesome

6. resolve   7. proposition   8. provoke   9. detract   10. solitary

11. hyperbole   12. providence   13. wary   14. conceive   15. consecrate

16. abduct

Names: <u>Lincoln Thoreau</u>

UNIT TEN

1:1

1. c   2. a   3. d   4. b   5. d

1:2

1. result   2. suited   3. revive   4. resume   5. previously

1:3

1. previously   2. revive   3. resume   4. result   5. suited

1:4

1. resume   2. suited   3. results   4. revive   5. previously

2:1

1. magnanimous   2. magnitude   3. -polis   4. mega-   5. -loqui

2:2

1. true   2. false   3. false   4. true   5. false

2:3

1. exactness   2. no   3. very small   4. no   5. exaggerating

3:1

1. b   2. c   3. a   4. c   5. b

3:2

1. variation   2. intend   3. reproduce   4. fluid   5. variation

6. fluid   7. range   8. reproduce   9. intend   10. range

3:3

1. intend   2. variation   3. reproduce   4. fluid   5. range

3:4

1. variation   2. reproduce   3. fluid   4. intend   5. range

4:1

1. auto-   2. autocrat   3. mobile   4. -nym   5. pseudonym

4:2

1. false   2. true   3. false   4. false   5. true

4:3

1. a   2. c   3. c   4. a   5. c

5:1

1. revive   2. reproduce   3. suit   4. revive   5. range

6. suit   7. reproduce   8. range

5:2

Answers will vary.

5:3

1. reproduce   2. imitate   3. revive   4. refresh   5. intend

6. plan

5:4

1. fluid   2. ranging   3. intended   4. suitable   5. result

6. revival   7. variety

5:5

ab- Prefix meaning from, away, or off.

abdicate *verb.* (1) To give up something, such as power or responsibility. (2) To resign; to give up a position or office.

abduct *verb.* To take a person away by force; kidnap.

absolute *adjective.* Total; complete.

absolutely *adverb.* (1) Completely. (2) Without a doubt.

absolve *verb.* To free someone from guilt, blame, responsibility or punishment.

abstain *verb.* (1) To hold back from. (2) To keep oneself from doing something.

abundance *noun.* A quantity that is greater than enough; plenty.

abundant *adjective.* Plentiful, ample.

acquaint *verb.* To become familiar with.

acquaintance *noun.* Person who is known, but who is not a close friend.

acquire *verb.* To come to possess; to obtain.

ad- Prefix meaning to or toward.

adapt *verb.* To make fit, often by making some changes.

adaptation *noun.* (1) The change that is made to make a thing fit a new purpose or space. (2) A change in an animal's structure or behavior to allow it to meet new conditions.

adept *adjective.* Highly skilled.

adhere *verb.* (1) To stick fast; to cling. (2) To support a person or an idea; to be loyal.

adherent *noun.* A person who believes strongly in and sticks by a particular leader, cause or idea.

adhesion *noun.* A thing that sticks; an attachment.

adhesive *noun.* A substance that glues or pastes things together.

adjacent (ə jā′ snt) *adjective.* Next to or close by.

administrator *noun.* One who manages or directs an organization.

adopt *verb.* (1) To choose. (2) To formally accept or approve. (3) To choose to raise as one's own a child born to other people. **adopted**

adoption *noun.* (1) The act of taking on by choice. (2) Formal acceptance; approval.

affix *verb.* To fasten or attach. **affixing**

affixed *adjective.* Fastened or attached.

agile (aj′əl) *adjective.* Able to move quickly and gracefully.

agility *noun.* Ability to move quickly and gracefully.

-animus Root meaning spirit.

anticipation *noun.* The act of looking forward to or expecting.

anticipatory *adjective.* Characterized by expectancy or looking forward.

antonym *noun.* A word of opposite meaning.

apprehend *verb.* (1) To seize. (2) To understand.

apt *adjective.* (1) Fitting or appropriate. (2) Likely.

assume *verb.* To suppose something to be true. **assumed**

attach *verb.* To fasten by a link, tie or bond.

attain *verb.* (1) To arrive at, come to, or reach. (2) To obtain.

For a guide to the pronunciation symbols used in this glossary, refer to *Scott, Foresman Advanced Dictionary.*

attainable *adjective*. (1) Reachable. (2) Possible to obtain.

attainment *noun*. The act of obtaining or reaching.

auto- Prefix meaning self.

autocrat *noun*. Ruler who claims complete power.

autograph *noun*. A person's signature.

automobile *noun*. A four-wheeled passenger car.

autonym *noun*. A person's real name.

autopsy (ô′top′sē) *noun*. The examination of a dead body to find the cause of death.

autosuggestion *noun*. The affecting of one's own behavior, attitudes or physical condition through unconscious mental means; self-hypnosis.

begin *verb*. To start.

bi-, bin- Prefix meaning two.

bicentennial *noun*. A two-hundredth anniversary.

binary *adjective*. Made up of two parts.

binary number system *noun*. A number system based on the numbers 0 and 1.

bisect *verb*. To cut in two.

boastful *adjective*. Tending to brag.

burden *noun*. Something carried; a heavy weight or load. *verb*. To put a heavy weight or load on a person, animal or thing.

calculate *verb*. To figure out.

catch *verb*. To seize something that is in flight or motion.

cautious *adjective*. Taking no chances; careful for the sake of safety.

civilized *adjective*. Showing culture and good manners; refined.

clarify *verb*. To make an idea understandable and clear.

clever *adjective*. Mentally quick.

closet *noun*. A closed room for storing things. *verb*. To shut oneself off in a room by oneself.

cognition *noun*. The act or process of knowing; knowledge.

com- Prefix meaning together, with or thoroughly.

combine *verb*. To bring two or more things together to form a new thing.

comfort *verb*. To bring strength and hope; to offer cheer.

comfortable *adjective*. Giving physical comfort, ease, contentment, or security.

complement *noun*. The amount needed to fill or complete something.

complete *adjective*. Finished, whole, full.

compliment *verb*. To give praise.

component *noun*. An individual part that goes into a product made up of a number of parts or elements.

compose *verb*. To put together, to make up, or to form.

composer *noun*. One who puts together, makes up, or forms something.

composite (kəm poz′it) *noun*. Something made up of several parts or elements.

composition *noun*. (1) The way in which something is put together. (2) A thing that has been assembled, or put together, such as an essay or a musical piece.

compound *noun.* A chemical product made up of individual elements.

con- Prefix meaning together.

conceive *verb.* To take into the mind; to think up. **conceived**

conception *noun.* The process of forming ideas.

conduct *verb.* (1) To lead or guide. (2) To carry out, or perform. (3) To transmit, receive or carry such things as electricity or heat. **conducted**

conductor *noun.* (1) Someone who leads or guides. (2) Anything that transmits or carries energy.

confer *verb.* To compare ideas.

conference *noun.* A meeting at which people discuss or compare ideas.

confine *verb.* To keep within limits; restrict; shut in. **confined**

confines *noun.* Boundary, border, limits.

congenial *adjective.* Agreeable; suitable to one's nature, taste or outlook.

congeniality *noun.* The quality of being agreeable, suitable, pleasant or sociable.

consecrate *verb.* (1) To devote to a purpose; dedicate. (2) To swear into office with a religious rite.

construe *verb.* To understand or explain the meaning or intention of something; interpret.

control *verb.* To have power over something.

convention *noun.* (1) A gathering of people for a particular purpose. (2) Custom; the generally agreed upon behavior of a group of people.

-crat Root meaning rule or power.

credit *noun.* A person or thing that brings honor or praise. *verb.* (1) To believe in the value of something. (2) To add to an account. **credited**

cult *noun.* (1) A group showing great admiration of a person, thing or idea. (2) Great admiration of a person, thing or idea.

curb *noun.* (1) Something that controls or restrains. (2) A border of concrete or stone along the edge of a sidewalk. *verb.* To hold in check; restrain.

de- Prefix meaning remove, the reverse of, reduce, get off, or do the opposite of.

decade *noun.* A period of ten years.

decide *verb.* To think out; to consider and then draw a conclusion.

decode *verb.* To translate, or take out of, code.

decompose *verb.* To rot or separate into basic elements, or ingredients.

deduce *verb.* To infer; to arrive at a conclusion through reasoning, or putting facts together.

deduct *verb.* To take away, to remove.

deduction *noun.* (1) An amount taken away from the total earned. (2) An inference or conclusion arrived at through reasoning.

delay *verb.* To put off; to postpone.

delineate *verb.* (1) To describe in detail. (2) To show or mark the outline of something. **delineating**

delineation *noun.* (1) The act of describing something in detail. (2) The act of pointing out or marking an outline. (3) A detailed description.

dem-, demos- Greek roots meaning the common people.

democracy *noun.* A form of government in which the people (and not royalty or a dictator) rule.

demure (di myür′) *adjective.* Being or appearing to be very modest, shy, quiet, or serious.

demurely *adverb.* In a modest, shy, reserved or serious manner.

derail *verb.* (1) To cause to go off the rails, or track.

derailleur (di rā′lər) *noun.* A spring-loaded mechanism on a bicycle that changes gears by causing the chain to move from one sprocket wheel to another.

-derm Greek root meaning skin or covering.

dermatologist *noun.* A skin doctor.

dermatology *noun.* The branch of science that studies the skin.

detect *verb.* To uncover; to find something that is hidden.

determine *verb.* To figure out the identity, character, scope, or direction of something.

detract *verb.* To take away something—often quality or worth.

devote *verb.* (1) To give all or most of one's attention to. (2) To give oneself over to a person or a cause.

devotion *noun.* Strong attachment or commitment shown by constant attention.

-dic Root meaning to proclaim, or say.

dictate *verb.* (1) To speak or read aloud to another person who writes down the spoken words. (2) To command or order.

dictator *noun.* A person who has total authority, especially a person who, through force, takes over a government.

diction *noun.* A person's manner of expressing ideas in words; a style of speaking or writing.

difficult *adjective.* Hard to do or understand.

diligence *noun.* Careful and steady effort.

diligently *adverb.* With careful and steady effort.

direct *adjective.* Straightforward; frank.

discipline *noun.* (1) Orderly and obedient behavior. (2) Punishment used to teach a lesson. *verb.* (1) To bring under control; to train. (2) To punish in order to correct or change behavior. **disciplined**

discontinue *verb.* Stop, put an end to or cease.

discontinuing *noun.* Stopping, putting an end to or ceasing from.

distinction *noun.* Mark of difference or identification.

distinctive *adjective.* Special; recognizably different.

distort *verb.* To twist out of a normal shape.

distribute *verb.* Scatter over a wide area.

duc- Latin root meaning to lead.

duct *noun.* A pipe or ditch that carries such things as air, water, or gas from one place to another.

easy *adjective.* Requiring little effort, thought or skill.

education *noun.* The development of knowledge or skill.

effect *noun.* The result or consequence of an action. *verb.* To bring about or cause to be.

effective *adjective.* Producing a desired result.

effectively *adverb.* In a manner that produces the desired result or consequences.

effects *noun.* Personal belongings or property.

efficiency *noun.* The quality of being productive without waste.

efficient *adjective.* Productive without waste.

eliminate *verb.* (1) To get rid of, to remove. (2) To leave out, omit. (3) To expel from the body.

eloquent (el′ə kwənt) *adjective.* Marked by strong, clear expression.

endure *verb.* (1) To suffer, to live through. (2) To bear without breaking; to last. **endured**

enduring *adjective.* Lasting, permanent.

enormity *noun.* Extreme wickedness.

epi- Prefix meaning upon, attached to, or over.

epicenter *noun.* The location on the earth's surface directly over the heart of an earthquake.

epidemic *noun.* (1) The widespread occurrence of a disease. (2) The outbreak or sudden spread of anything. *adjective.* Affecting many people in a population.

epidemiology *noun.* The branch of medicine that studies how diseases occur in and affect populations.

epidermis *noun.* The outer layer of skin.

epigraph *noun.* (1) An engraved inscription. (2) A quotation, often found at the beginning of a book, that hints at the book's theme.

epitaph *noun.* An inscription, as on a gravestone, or a brief statement, in memory of someone who has died.

ex- Prefix meaning out of, from or former.

excavate *verb.* (1) To dig out; to dig a hole; to hollow something out. (2) To expose by digging away a covering.

excavation *noun.* (1) The act of digging a hole or of uncovering something by digging away a covering. (2) A site where people are digging away earth or uncovering something by digging away a covering.

exceed *verb.* (1) To surpass, outdo; go over the limit or record. (2) To go beyond the limit set by authority or custom. **exceeded**

excel *verb.* To be or do better than others. **excelled**

excellent *adjective.* Superior; very good of its kind.

excess *noun.* Beyond measure; more than is needed.

exclude *verb.* To shut out or keep out.

exclusive *adjective.* (1) Not shared with others. (2) Shutting others out.

execute *verb.* (1) To carry out, do. (2) To put to death according to law. **exceeding, exceeded**

execution *noun.* The act of carrying out or performing.

exert *verb.* To put forth; to bring to bear; use. **exerting**

exertion *noun.* The act of putting forth strength.

exhale *verb.* To breathe out.

expire *verb.* (1) To come to an end. (2) To die. (3) To breathe out.

explode *verb.* To burst apart with a loud noise; to blow up.

export *noun.* A product sent out of a country. *verb.* To send something out of a country.

-fer Latin root meaning to carry or bear.

fere- Latin root meaning to strike.

final *adjective.* Defined end point.

first *adjective.* Coming before all others in time, order or importance.

fix *verb.* (1) To attach or fasten firmly, to make stable. (2) To focus steadily. **fixed**

fixed *adjective.* Stationary, immovable; unchanging.

fixedly *adverb.* Without movement.

fixture *noun.* (1) Anything placed in a firm position. (2) Something which is attached to a house or building.

fluid *noun.* Liquid, gas, or anything that flows. *adjective.* Flowing; like a liquid or gas.

fluidity *noun.* Capability of flowing.

fold *verb.* (1) To bring to an end; to go out of business. (2) Bend or double over itself. **folded, folding**

formalize *verb.* To make official. **formalized**

formally *adverb.* (1) Officially, with ceremony. (2) Precisely; according to set rules.

forte (fôr′tā) *adverb.* Musical term meaning in a loud or forceful manner.

fulfill *verb.* To carry out or to live up to something, as a dream or promise.

fulfilled *adjective.* Satisfied, content.

fulfillment *noun.* (1) The realization or accomplishment of something. (2) Contentment, satisfaction.

graduate *verb.* (1) To pass from one stage or level to a higher one. (2) To finish a course of study at a school. (3) To mark out in equal spaces for measuring. **graduated**

graduation *noun.* The ceremony marking the completion of a course of study.

graph- Root meaning to write.

humble *adjective.* Not grand, lofty or noble; modest and unassuming.

humility *noun.* A feeling of one's own insignificance, or smallness.

hyper- Prefix meaning over, above, beyond or too much.

hyperacidity *noun.* Having too much acid, especially in the stomach.

hyperactive *adjective.* Overly active.

hyperbole (hī pėr′bə lē) *noun.* Exaggeration of expression, as in "eyes as big as saucers."

hypercritical *adjective.* Excessively critical.

hypermnesia (hī′pərm nē′zhə) *noun.* An abnormally complete or vivid memory of past events.

hypersensitive *adjective.* (1) Abnormally affected by criticism; overly sensitive. (2) Abnormally sensitive to certain drugs or germs.

hypersonic *adjective.* Moving at a speed five times faster than the speed of sound.

hyperspace *noun.* Space of more than three dimensions.

il-, ill- Prefix meaning not.

ill-advised *adjective.* Showing a lack of wise counsel and advice; not advised.

illegal *adjective.* Not legal.

illegible *adjective.* Incapable of being deciphered or read.

ill-humored *adjective.* Irritable, grouchy; in a bad mood.

illiteracy *noun.* The inability to read and write.

illiterate *adjective.* Being unable to read and write.

illogical *adjective.* Not reasonable or correctly thought out; not following the rules of logic.

im- Latin prefix meaning not or in.

imagine *verb.* To visualize a plan, idea or thought.

imbibe *verb.* (1) To drink in; to absorb. (2) To take in liquid.

imitate *verb.* (1) To try to be like or act like someone else. (2) To follow a pattern or model. **imitating**

immobile *adjective.* Incapable of being moved; not mobile.

impartial *adjective.* Showing no more favor to one side than to another; fair, just.

impartiality *noun.* Fairness, justice; the act of treating all equally and without bias.

implode *verb.* (1) To burst inward. (2) To collapse inward as if from outside pressure.

import *noun.* An object that is brought in to one place from another place, usually a foreign country. *verb.* To bring in, usually from a foreign place.

improper *adjective.* Not in accord with modesty, manners or good taste.

in- Prefix meaning in, not, or the opposite of.

inability *noun.* The lack of sufficient power, resources or capability.

incapable *adjective.* Lacking sufficient power, resources or capability.

inclination *noun.* A natural tendency or preference; a liking.

inclined *adjective.* (1) Favorable or willing; having a tendency. (2) Sloping or slanted.

incognito (in'kog nē'tō) *adjective.* With one's identity hidden.

incorporate *verb.* (1) To make something part of something else, to join or combine. (2) To form into a legal group of merchants, traders, or businesses. **incorporating**

incorporation *noun.* (1) The act of making something a part of something else. (2) The act of becoming a legal group of merchants, traders, or businesses.

increase *noun.* The act of making greater in size, amount, number or intensity. *verb.* To make greater in size, amount, number or intensity.

indicate *verb.* To point out; show.

indication *noun.* (1) The act of showing or pointing out. (2) That which points out; that which signifies.

indoors *adverb.* In or into a building.

infer *verb.* To arrive at a conclusion based on the available evidence or information.

inference *noun.* A conclusion reached by observing the available information or evidence.

inhabit *verb.* To live in.

inhabitant *noun.* A person or animal that lives in a place.

inhabited *adjective.* Lived in.

inhale *verb.* To breathe in.

inject *verb.* (1) To force a fluid into (as for medical purposes). (2) To introduce a new idea or element into something.

injection *noun.* (1) An act of forcing a fluid into something for medical purposes. (2) The act of introducing a new element into something.

innate *adjective.* A talent or quality born in a person rather than learned over time; natural.

innately *adverb.* By nature; present from birth.

inspire *verb.* (1) To move or guide by supernatural means. (2) To make lively; to spur on. (3) To inhale.

intelligent *adjective.* Having a high degree of mental ability.

intend *verb.* To have in mind as a particular purpose, to plan. **intended, intending**

intention *noun.* A purpose or plan one has in mind.

inter- Latin prefix meaning between or among.

interaction *noun.* Mutual action or influence between two or more people or things.

intercept *verb.* To take or seize something that is on its way from one place to another.

interfere *verb.* (1) To block or get in the way of; to obstruct. (2) To poke into other people's business.

interference *noun.* (1) The act of getting in the way of. (2) The act of poking into the affairs of others.

interject *verb.* To insert between or into other things.

interlude *noun.* (1) Something that fills the time between two other things. (2) A short piece of music, usually played between two longer pieces or between the acts of a play.

international *adjective.* Having to do with two or more nations.

interpret *verb.* (1) To explain. (2) To come to your own understanding.

interrogate *verb.* To question thoroughly to obtain information.

interrogation *noun.* A formal questioning.

interrogation point *noun.* A question mark.

interrogative *adjective.* Having the form or force of a question.

interrogator *noun.* A person who asks questions formally to obtain information.

intersect *verb.* (1) To divide by passing through or across. (2) To meet and cross at a point.

intersection *noun.* A place where two or more things, such as roads, cross.

interstellar *adjective.* Among the stars.

interval *noun.* A given amount of time or space between events.

invigorate *verb.* To fill with life and energy.

invigorating *adjective.* Filled with life and energy.

isolation *noun.* The state of being detached from others.

issue *noun.* (1) A debated point or matter of importance. *verb.* (1) To put into circulation; deliver for use.

lack *noun.* Something that is missing or is needed. *verb.* To be missing something; to be in need of something.

last *adjective.* Coming after all others in time, order or importance.

latter (lat′ər) *adjective.* The last item mentioned in a series.

legible *adjective.* Plain and clear; easy to read.

ligament *noun.* A tough body tissue that connects bones or holds organs in place.

-ligate Latin root meaning to bind.

limit *noun.* A boundary or restricting feature. *verb.* To assign boundaries to something; to restrict.

-liter Latin root meaning letter.

literate *adjective.* (1) Able to read and write. (2) Well-read; having read a great deal about many subjects; educated.

literature *noun.* Writings, such as books and stories, especially those that have lasting value because of their fineness of expression and the wide interest of the ideas they express.

loquacious (lō kwā′shəs) *adjective.* Talkative.

-loqui Root meaning speech.

magnanimous *adjective.* Unselfish, generous, noble.

magni- Prefix meaning to make larger.

magnify *verb.* To enlarge; to cause to look larger.

magniloquent (mag nil′ə kwənt) *adjective.* Using large words; speaking in an overly grand manner.

magnitude *noun.* (1) Great size. (2) Size regardless of largeness or smallness. (3) Importance.

maniac *noun.* An insane person.

marina (mə rē′nə) *noun.* A dock or harbor where small boats can moor and where supplies and repair facilities are usually available.

marine *adjective.* Of the sea.

mariner (mar′ə nər) *noun.* A seaman or sailor.

mega- Greek prefix meaning great, large or one million.

megalomania *noun.* A false sense of personal power and importance.

megalomaniac *noun.* Someone who suffers from a false sense of personal power and importance.

megalopolis *noun.* A huge city, or a thickly populated area consisting of several large cities.

mere *adjective.* Being nothing more than.

merely *adverb.* Simply, solely; for this and no other purpose.

-merge Root meaning to plunge or dive.

merge *verb.* (1) To combine into one. (2) To cause one thing (often a business) to be absorbed or swallowed up by another, so that the smaller thing loses its identity, simply becoming part of the larger.

merger *noun.* A combining of two or more things (often businesses) into one.

metro- Root meaning womb or uterus.

minister *noun.* (1) A member of the clergy. (2) A person in charge of a department of the government. *verb.* To give aid or service (as to the sick).

mis- Prefix meaning badly, wrongly or the opposite of something.

misapprehension *noun.* A misunderstanding.

miscalculate *verb.* To figure out incorrectly.

misconceive *verb.* To understand something wrongly.

misconception *noun.* An incorrect understanding.

misconstrue *verb.* To misunderstand an intention as conveyed by speech or action.

misinterpret *verb.* To come to an incorrect understanding.

misinterpretation *noun.* An incorrect understanding of the facts at hand.

mit Root meaning send.

mobile *noun.* A moving sculpture of objects suspended on wires or threads. *adjective.* Easy to move.

modest *adjective.* Being moderate about one's capabilities or worth.

non- Prefix meaning not, the opposite of, or the lack of.

nonprofit *adjective.* Not conducted or maintained for the purpose of making money over and above costs.

nonsense *noun.* Talk or action that does not make sense, that is foolish or silly.

nonviolence *noun.* (1) The avoidance of violence as a matter of principle. (2) The belief in using peaceful methods for solving problems.

notify *verb.* To make others aware of information or news.

-nox Root meaning to harm.

noxious (nok'shəs) *adjective.* Harmful to health or life; poisonous.

ob- Prefix meaning in the way of, against or toward.

obedient *adjective.* Tending to follow the directions or commands of those in authority.

object *verb.* To express an opinion against an idea or action.

objectionable *adjective.* Disagreeable, offensive or unpleasant.

objective *noun.* A goal that seems capable of being reached.

obligate *verb.* To make responsible; to hold one to one's promise.

obligated *adjective.* Responsible for; bound to do by law or because of a promise.

obliterate *verb.* (1) To get rid of or destroy entirely; erase. (2) To blot out or cover over entirely.

oblong *adjective.* Longer in one dimension, as in a long loaf of bread, an egg shape, or a rectangle.

obnoxious (ob nok'shəs) *adjective.* Disagreeable; highly offensive; annoying.

offset *verb.* (1) To make up or compensate for. (2) To show to advantage. (3) To balance. **offsetting**

opponent *noun.* One who is against something.

origin *noun.* (1) The beginning, the starting point. (2) The thing from which anything comes.

originate *verb.* (1) Come into being or begin. (2) Cause to be, invent. **originated**

over- Prefix meaning above, across, too much or extra.

overcome *verb.* (1) Make weak, powerless or helpless. (2) Get the better of; defeat.

overdress *verb.* (1) To dress too warmly. (2) To dress too well or elaborately for a social occasion.

overhead *adverb.* Above one's head.

overlook *verb.* To miss or omit because of neglect.

overmatch *verb.* To match or pair unequally against an opponent stronger or more able than the other.

oversee *verb.* (1) To manage or direct the work of other people. (2) To look over from a high position.

overseer *noun.* A person who manages or directs the work of other people.

oversight *noun.* A failure to notice or see something; the omission of something that should have been seen, done or included.

overstate *verb.* To express something too strongly; exaggerate.

overstatement *noun.* Exaggeration.

overwhelm *verb.* To overpower or upset someone by being too great, strong, heavy or difficult.

overwhelming *adjective.* Great; much more than expected; too heavy or too much to cope with; overpowering.

pause *noun.* A temporary stop in action.

peculiar *adjective.* Characteristic of one thing or type of thing.

phonograph *noun.* A record player.

photograph *noun.* A picture made with a camera. *verb.* To take pictures with a camera.

plan *verb.* To think out beforehand how something is to be done.

-polis Root meaning city.

-port Latin root meaning to carry.

port *noun.* A place where ships anchor or dock.

porter *noun.* A person who carries things for others.

pose *verb.* (1) To present or set forth (as a question). (2) To hold or place in a certain position. **poses, posing**

posture *noun.* (1) The position of the body or the manner of holding the body. (2) The condition, situation or state of something.

pre- Prefix meaning before.

preatomic *adjective.* Describing the time before the use of atomic energy and the atom bomb.

precede *verb.* To go before in time or order.

preclude *verb.* To shut out or rule out in advance; to prevent or make impossible.

precognition *noun.* Knowing something before it happens.

precook *verb.* To cook part way before finally cooking, or before reheating.

predict *verb.* To tell in advance that something is going to happen.

prefer *verb.* To like one thing or person more than another.

prefix *noun.* The part of a word that is fixed or attached in front of the root.

prehistoric *adjective.* Before the time when people started writing about the events of their times; before written history.

prejudice *verb.* To form an opinion without taking the time and care to judge fairly; to judge before knowing all the facts.

prevail *verb.* (1) To gain a victory through strength. (2) To use persuasion effectively. (3) To be in fashion or widespread use.
  prevailed, prevailing

prevent *verb.* To keep from happening; to hold or keep back.

previous *adjective.* Coming before or earlier in time.

previously *adverb.* At an earlier time.

pro- Prefix meaning before or in favor of.

procedure *noun.* (1) A series of steps followed in a regular, definite order. (2) A way of accomplishing something.

proceed *verb.* (1) To move forward. (2) To carry on with an activity.

proclaim *verb.* To declare something publicly in speech or writing.

proclamation *noun.* (1) The act of making a public declaration. (2) A public declaration in speech or writing.

procrastinate *verb.* To put things off until a later time.

procrastination *noun.* The act of putting things off until a later time.

produce (prod′ üs) *noun.* Fruits and vegetables; crops. *verb.* (prə düs′) To create, exhibit or manufacture.

producer *noun.* One who makes, creates or manufactures something.

propel *verb.* To drive forward by a force that creates motion.

propeller *noun.* A device consisting of a central hub and revolving blades that is attached to boats and aircraft to drive the vehicles forward.

proponent *noun.* One who is in favor of something.

proposal *noun.* (1) An act of putting something forth for consideration. (2) Something put forth for consideration.

proposition *noun.* (1) A statement presented as being true. (2) A statement presented for consideration or approval.

propulsion *noun.* A force or impulse that drives an object or vehicle forward.

protest (pro′ test) *noun.* A statement that denies or disagrees with an idea or action. *verb.* (prâ test′) To make a statement or gesture against an idea or action.

provide *verb.* To prepare for a need.

providence *noun.* (1) Divine guidance or care. (2) The state of being prepared for the future.

provident *adjective.* Making careful plans for the future.

provision *noun.* (1) The act of providing with supplies. (2) A stock of needed supplies. *verb.* To supply with food and materials.

provoke *verb.* (1) To excite into action. (2) To call forth a response by word or deed.

pseudonym (süd′n im) *noun.* A false name used by a celebrity, criminal or author; a pen name.

push *verb.* To press against with force in order to move something or someone.

range *noun.* The extent of variations within set limits. *verb.* To vary within certain limits.
  ranged, ranging

rare *adjective*. (1) Seldom seen or found. (2) Cooked so that the inside is still red (as in meat).

rarely *adverb*. Hardly ever; infrequently.

re- Prefix meaning back or again.

recede *verb*. (1) To move back or away; withdraw. (2) To grow less or smaller.

recess *noun*. (1) A short intermission between periods of work or school. (2) A cavity in a wall that is set back, or in, from the rest of the wall. *verb*. To suspend work or school for relaxation.

recluse *noun*. A person who chooses to live alone, apart from society.

recount *verb*. (1) To count again. (2) To tell about something, such as an event, in detail.

redo *verb*. To do again.

reduce *verb*. (1) Make less or smaller, decrease. (2) Change to another form. (3) Bring to a certain state, or condition. **reduced**

reduction *noun*. The act of lessening or making smaller.

refresh *verb*. To bring new strength or energy to something or someone. **refreshed**

reject *verb*. (1) To throw back. (2) To refuse to accept, consider or submit to. **rejected**

relation *noun*. A quality that connects two or more things or people.

relative *adjective*. In comparison or in reference to.

relatively *adverb*. Comparatively; to a degree, somewhat.

remedy *noun*. A means of relieving disease; a cure. *verb*. To put right; to cure. **remedied**

remit *verb*. To send payment for something that has been bought.

removal *noun*. The act of getting rid of something by moving it from one place to another.

remove *verb*. Get rid of; eliminate. **removed**

removed *adjective*. At a distance from; separate or distant in space or time.

renew *verb*. (1) To restore something to freshness or vigor. (2) To restore something to its original state.

repair *verb*. To fix something that is broken.

repay *verb*. To pay back.

replica *noun*. A copy or reproduction of something.

replicate *verb*. To make a replica, or copy, of something.

reply *verb*. To respond or answer.

report *noun*. A written or spoken account of an event.

reproduce *verb*. (1) To make an identical copy. (2) To produce offspring. **reproduced**

resolute *adjective*. Marked by firm determination.

resolution *noun*. (1) An answer; a solution to a problem. (2) A formal opinion or decision made by a group such as a governing body or an organization.

resolve *verb*. (1) To settle a question or solve a problem. (2) To make up one's mind to accomplish something.

restoration *noun*. Renewal; repairing of damages or injuries done.

restore *verb.* To return something to its original condition. **restored**

result *noun.* Something that is caused to happen; an outcome. *verb.* To follow as a consequence. **resulted, resulting**

resume *verb.* To begin again; go on from where one left off. **resumed**

retract *verb.* (1) To take back. (2) To draw back.

revival *noun.* A bringing back to life, consciousness or awareness.

revive *verb.* (1) To bring back into fashion or use. (2) To bring back or come back to life or consciousness. **revived**

revolve *verb.* To move in a curved path around an axis.

roga- Latin root meaning to ask.

scribe Root meaning to write.

seasoned *adjective.* Grown experienced over a period of time.

seclusion *noun.* The state of being shut away from others.

-sect Latin root meaning to cut or divide.

secure *verb.* (1) To take possession of something. (2) To fasten firmly.

security *noun.* (1) Freedom from danger; feeling or condition of being safe. (2) Something that assures safety.

shrewd *adjective.* Clever; of good judgment.

skilled *adjective.* Having mastered a technique or skill.

snare *noun.* A trap that entangles a bird or other small animals. *verb.* To capture with a trap. **snared**

solitary *adjective.* Alone; without companionship.

solitude *noun.* The state of being alone.

solve Root meaning to loosen.

solve *verb.* To find the answer to a puzzle or problem.

solvent *noun.* A substance that can dissolve other substances.

sprightly *adjective.* Having a lively, brisk quality.

steal *verb.* To move secretly or quietly. **stolen**

stern *adjective.* Severe or serious looking; harsh.

stolen *adjective.* Taken away by force or unjust means.

strain *noun.* A severe pressure, weight or force. *verb.* To injure by exerting too much effort or by stretching too far.

strenuous *adjective.* Requiring much energy and stamina.

sub- Latin prefix meaning under.

submerge *verb.* (1) To sink under water. (2) To put something under water or to cover something with water.

submissive *noun.* Yielding to the power or control of another; obedient.

submit *verb.* To deliver formally; to turn in or give over.

subscribe *verb.* (1) To promise to accept and pay for something. (2) To approve or agree.

subscriber *noun.* A person who formally agrees to accept and pay for something.

subscription *noun.* An agreement to accept and pay for something; the right to receive something that will be paid for.

subtract *verb.* To take away.

succumb *verb.* To yield to a greater strength or force, such as disease or death. **succumbed**

suit *noun.* (1) A case in a court of law. (2) An application to a court to file a case. *verb.* (1) To make fit or appropriate. (2) To be appropriate for; agree with.

suitable *adjective.* Right for the occasion; fitting or appropriate.

suited *adjective.* Appropriate or fitting.

sustenance *noun.* A means of supporting life; food and supplies.

synonym *noun.* One of two or more words that have the same or nearly the same meaning.

-test Root meaning to witness or testify.

think *verb.* To have an idea enter one's mind.

-tract Root meaning to remove by drawing back.

trans- Latin prefix meaning across or beyond.

transfer *noun.* The carrying of information or an object from one place to another. *verb.* To carry or send something from one place to another.

transport *verb.* To carry something from one place to another.

trial *noun.* A process for testing or examining.

tribulation *noun.* Great trouble or distress.

troupe *noun.* A group or company of people, particularly performers.

try *verb.* (1) To test; push to the limit. (2) To attempt; to undertake. **tried**

trying *adjective.* Testing one's strength or patience to the limit.

-tude A suffix that indicates the state or quality of the word it is attached to.

ultimate *adjective.* Last, best or utmost.

ultimately *adverb.* In the end; finally.

ultimatum *noun.* A final offer or demand expressed with an accompanying threat of penalty.

un- Prefix meaning not or the opposite of.

unbiased *adjective.* Free from prejudice and favoritism; fair.

uncivilized *adjective.* (1) Not civilized; savage; wild. (2) Not following the social customs of society.

uncommon *adjective.* Occurring infrequently; out of the ordinary.

understudy *noun.* A person who is trained to act as a substitute for a regular performer. *verb.* To study another actor's part in order to be able to substitute in an emergency.

unique *adjective.* One of a kind; having no like or equal.

uniqueness *noun.* The quality of having no like or equal.

variation *noun.* A somewhat different form of something.

variety *noun.* A number of different kinds of something.

various *adjective.* Of differing kinds.

vary *verb.* (1) To make changes in the order or structure of something. (2) To be different from one time to the next.

versatile *adjective.* Able to do many things well.

versatility *noun.* The ability to do many things well.

versed *adjective.* Experienced or skilled.

-vide Root meaning see.

vigor *noun.* Healthy energy or power; active strength.

vigorous *adjective.* Having power and energy.

wariness *noun.* The quality of being on guard against danger.

warp *verb.* (1) To distort; to lead or turn from good to bad. (2) To bend or twist out of shape.

wary *adjective.* On guard against danger; cautious or careful.

-whelm Root meaning to cover up.

wholesome *adjective.* Healthful or beneficial; good for the body, mind or morals.